# The Man
# from Baghdad

Widad E. Bazzoui, M.D.

The Man From Baghdad
Copyright 2018
ISBN: 978-0-9993415-9-9 paperback, Memoir

These are my memories of growing up in a loving Iraqi family in
Baghdad. It is all true to the best of my recollections. WB

Editor: Cynthia L. Moyer
Cover art: Pretty AF Designs
CB Publishing
Printed in the USA

# Table of Contents

# Prologue

My life in Baghdad had a sweetness and tranquility. My family home had a warm and loving ambience. I remember Iraq as an ancient, yet youthful country; its boundaries established by the Allies after World War I. It was reaching for a place in the civilized world.

The peacefulness—even with the lack of equality—the neighborliness, and the serenity are now long gone and, in their place, is hate, fear, and an unabated thirst for revenge.

I was born when Iraq was still a kingdom. As Christians, we were the largest religious minority at the time. The level of education was slightly below what existed in the educated countries of Europe, yet, I believe—and many of my fellow Iraqis would agree—that for us, those were great days. Look at what we have now: war, hatred, religious persecution, corruption, desire for revenge, and lots of money, poorly managed.

When I was growing up, the royal family of Iraq came to us from Hejaz, in the northern part of what is now Saudi Arabia. When the British started getting closer to the Middle East in the first World War, they convinced Grand Sharif Hussein bin Ali to rise against the Ottoman Empire and promised to help him continue his rule over that part of Arabia. Hussein, king of Hejaz and descendent of the Hashemite tribe, was highly respected by the people of Arabia. Britain won the war and was given reign over Iraq, Jordan and Palestine. They decided to install

# Widad E. Bazzoui

Hussein's second son as the King of Iraq, Faisal I. King Faisal took over in 1921 and did a decent job putting together a government with a parliament, prime minister, ministers, and even a small army.

Before the dissolution of the Ottoman Empire, the Fertile Crescent, the Levant, and Mesopotamia were names used interchangeably to describe the Arabic-speaking Middle East. The land was a heterogeneous spread of property that about seven to eight thousand years ago was a verdant fertile land that was a source of beauty and richness for the people who stumbled upon it.

Over the centuries, it gradually transformed into what it is now. It was the crossroad of diverse cultures, languages, traditions and religions. For four hundred years it was ruled by the Ottomans. The diverse terrain covered rivers, fertile prairies, mountains and a vast desert in the south. It allowed easy and open interconnections, unhindered by boundaries, religions, or tribal entities. The predominant language for the last fifteen hundred years has been Arabic. Islam is the religion of the majority. For centuries, Islam, Jews and Christians learned to coexist with each other, maintaining a more or less peaceable relationship while respecting each other's differences.

It was a difficult decision for me to write the story of my early years in Iraq; describing facets of the culture and family that no longer exist. It was at the urging of my wife, and my desire to share my history with my daughters, that I finally decided to write about the land from where their father came, and about the events of my early life in Baghdad and beyond. I hope my memories will be of interest to other readers as well.

*Dedicated to my sister, Nadia Bazzoui LeBanc.*
*Since she was, unfortunately, not there*
*to share many of these memories with us.*

# Chapter One

# The Beginning

My family name is Bazzoui. My father told me that at one time the name was Bo'a. How and why the name Bo'a changed to Bazzoui is beyond me. My grandfather Thomas (called Toma), worked in Basra as the postmaster of that city. At some earlier time, he used the name Khayat (which means tailor), as the name of his grandfather. He had five children: Antoin, Matilda, Emile (my father), Emilia, and finally Joseph.

My grandmother was Jameela Ni'mani Tappooni. She came from a distinguished family that produced the first cardinal in Chaldean Catholic Church, who was her maternal uncle. My father's family, not to be surpassed, produced a patriarch of the Chaldean Catholic Church, who reigned over all the Chaldean churches in the east and west. He took the religious name of Abdisho', which, translated from the Chaldean language, means the servant of Jesus. He was my father's paternal uncle. These days titles do not mean much, but a hundred and fifty years ago, they carried great honor and influence.

Unfortunately, my grandmother died during the childbirth of my Uncle Joseph, leaving Toma in a sad and difficult conundrum. He had to keep his job, but he also had to take care of the five children, so he decided to take his children to Baghdad where he had family. The family arranged to have a retired brother-in-law, along with the rest of the family, raise the children. Toma kept his job and traveled back and forth on weekends to spend time with his children, who had great affection for him. And when he retired, he moved back to Baghdad and lived with us until his death.

My father, Emile, was third in the sibling line. When he was six, he was enrolled in a French school run by the brothers of the Dominican Order. He told us when we were growing up that he graduated with a high-school education. As was done at the time, he met the requirements to become a lawyer by apprenticeship. His legal career was interrupted by his eagerness to help overturn the Ottoman Empire which had colonized Iraq for four hundred years.

He then joined a secret society that was conspiring to overthrow the government of Iraq, "Iraq Al Fatat," which translated means "Iraq the Maiden." Unfortunately for him and a friend of his, a fiery letter they were sending to some new recruits was intercepted. My father's letters were of such a serious nature that he was arrested and sentenced to die. His friend was lucky. He was sentenced to exile in a remote part of the country. As it happened, my grandfather, who still held a high-ranking position in the government, interceded for my father, and the sentence was commuted to exile, like his friend.

While he was in jail, his father arranged for my father, Emile, through bribery, to leave the jail and go to the house of Emile's older sister, Matilda Bazzoui Obaji, every night to wash, eat, and sleep. He was supposed to be back in jail early in the morning. One day when he was returning to jail, he witnessed a funeral procession passing in the street, as was customary at that time when an important person was being buried. He stopped and asked a man standing in the large group of spectators who the dead person was. To his surprise he was told that it was the funeral of a hanged man whose name was also Emile Bazzoui! My father crossed himself, lowered his head and sneaked back to jail having witnessed "his" own funeral.

One morning, four horsemen came to the jail to escort the two traitors to their exile. They'd brought two horses for the jailed conspirators. The trip was long and painful since neither of the two "criminals" had until then ridden in earnest. By the evening, after a grueling and long journey, they arrived at their destination, where they were exiled for the rest of their lives: A small mountainous village called Mandali, a poor, arid, and isolated village far away from civilization. They lived in a hut and learned to fend for themselves. They were supported by funds sent from time to time by their respective families.

In 1917, the British were making their way north from Basra in an effort to occupy Iraq. My father and his friend received word about this and started conspiring to escape and head in the direction of the advancing British troops.

They looked for a reliable guide to take them as far south as he could, hoping to meet the advancing Brits. After a long search, they found someone they could trust who knew the area. They set out on three horses late one night. After four or five hours of a rough and frightening ride, climbing hillocks and wading in streams, they arrived at a small Bedouin encampment. With great trepidation they stopped and asked to speak with the head of the tribe. As is the tradition of the Bedouins, the sheikh welcomed them and asked the women of his family to prepare food and a tent for the guests.

Over the centuries, the Arabs have lived with the tradition of hospitality. Any guest who seeks food or shelter is to be given shelter and protection for as long as he is their guest. Because of the nature of their Bedouin life, a system developed based on honor and shame to accommodate travelers in the desert. They try to feed guests with what they can provide. If they fail in this duty, they stand to lose their honor and good name among the neighboring tribes.

After my father and his companions ate bread, dates, and yogurt, they went to their tent to sleep with the understanding that they would be leaving shortly after midnight. A short time later, a young girl sneaked into the tent and whispered to my father that her father, the sheikh, had ordered some of his gunmen to ambush them after they leave. The guide was alarmed and decided that they should stay until the morning, but my father and his friend were anxious to leave as a soon as possible.

They asked the guide if he knew a different way to go. After thinking about it, he told them that other routes were even more dangerous. After serious deliberation, the three silently saddled their horses and left much earlier than they had planned.

Within an hour of riding in the dark, they heard men screaming at them to stop or be shot. In the moonlight, they saw several armed men appearing from behind the rocks, pointing their guns at them. The three riders stopped and got off their horses as they were told. Before long, the three horsemen were gazing at each other completely naked, with no money, no horses, and no weapons. Everything they counted on to tide them over until they got to safety was gone. The guide told them that they were within a few hours of their destination. So, totally naked, they started walking.

As dawn was breaking, they came to the outskirts of a small town southeast of Baghdad. In those days the women came out to the river very early to bathe and wash their clothes, before the men woke up. Suddenly three naked men covering their genitals with their hands appeared from nowhere. The women started screaming and covering themselves and running to their cottages. This created a dangerous situation for the three young men. The men of the village came out with guns to see who had violated the modesty of their women and the religious rules of their tribe. This was no simple violation of tribal law, or the Islamic code. The men were ready to shoot these intruders.

My father, never moving his hands, pleaded for mercy and asked for help; he explained to the angry men who they were, and why they were in such a disgraceful state. Fortunately, the British had already arrived in that area. The three men were directed to the army's headquarters, which was also the commander's living quarters. They sat outside waiting for the morning to break. After an hour, a sergeant came out of the house only to stare at the three naked men, two of whom spoke English fluently.

They asked if they could see the commander. After giving them clothes, they were taken to see the major who found the situation amusing. The major gave my father and his friend some money and they found their way back to Baghdad.

Soon after the British occupation began in 1917, my father was offered a job in Hilla where he remained for several years as an interpreter and assistant to the British military governor of central Iraq. While there, he established a small business for himself. He traded in commodities such as dates, date syrup, sheep skins, rice, etc. He also bought and sold Arabian horses. My father worked very hard for many years in that position. Finally, he felt that he had made enough money to travel to Europe and see the world. He decided to take a "Grand Tour" of Europe in 1925-26.

My father's brother-in-law, Matilda's husband, Joseph Obaji, gave Emile a lot of information about the trip, having done business with many foreign countries. He was encouraged, on his way back from Europe, to visit Joseph Obaji's family in Aleppo, Syria, where his brother-in-law had been born and raised. Joseph had given him the names of his brothers who were very well known and from a rather well-to-do family there.

# The Man from Baghdad

My father traveled from Baghdad to Damascus, then to Lebanon and from there to Greece by ship. For many years I heard him describing the wonders of the Greek Islands and the beauty of the Greek women. "Imagine," he would say, "they were swimming in the Mediterranean Sea half-clad in the company of men."

Of course, for a man coming from a backward country, as Iraq was at that time, with its women covered from head to toe and totally segregated from men, this was mind boggling and contrary to the moral edicts of "any religion." Not only did he have a jolting experience in Greece, but he almost lost his bearings when arriving in Paris. He witnessed some shocking examples of mankind's slide into utter immorality. With his two eyes he saw men and women kissing shamelessly on the Champs-Elysées.

This is not to say that given half a chance he would not have gladly emulated those lucky couples.

One of the great memories that his nephews and nieces have of this trip was the marvelous gifts he brought back for them. But after having satisfied himself with the joys of Europe, it was time for him to go back to the Arabic-speaking countries.

My father spoke and wrote fluently in Turkish, French, and Arabic—his native language. Since the Ottoman Empire had colonized the region for more than three centuries, Turkish was the official language of most Arab countries. In addition, he was fluent in English from working and translating for the British. Having all these languages at his command, he had an easy time during that trip.

On his way back home, he decided to go to Aleppo, Syria, as was recommended to him by his brother-in-law. He was going to visit the Obaji brothers and meet many of the distinguished members of the Christian community. The Obajis received their brother's brother-in-law with much fanfare. After all, he himself belonged to a well-known and respected Christian family in Iraq. They took him to see the city and its sights. They wined and dined him. On Sunday, they took him to church. It was there that he met many of the well-known and respectable Christian families of Aleppo.

At the time, Aleppo was the second largest and most prosperous city in Syria. It is also one of the oldest cities in the world. Not only was it on the Silk Road that carried all the goods heading to Europe from China, but it was also in the path of all the European invaders who came to the Middle East. Each invading nation had an agenda as they conquered and settled in Syria and Palestine.

And it was in Aleppo that my father met the Homseys, my mother's family. Her father's name was Joseph Homsey, her three brothers were Antione, George, and Shafeeq, and her two sisters were named Olga and Rose. From the moment he saw Mary he was interested in getting to know her. She was a beautiful blonde with green eyes and a light complexion. I understand it was a mutual interest.

He asked his hosts if they could arrange a visit to the Homseys to get to know the family. The visit was arranged. Many more visits followed, and he and Mary found themselves falling in love. Emile asked her father for her hand in marriage. The Obajis were known to the Homseys. They vouched for my father's family and his standing in the community, as well as his personal trustworthiness. Mary's mother had been deceased for some years. Her father, with the council of his children, gave his blessing to the proposal.

Because of the forbidding distance between Aleppo and Baghdad, they had a brief engagement ceremony after which my father returned to Baghdad. Preparations for the wedding started with letters going back and forth. To bring a bride from another country to a new environment was an anxiety-provoking task for the families of the bride as well as the bridegroom. A house in Baghdad had to be furnished anew. My father lived in Hilla. All his belongings had to be moved, thrown out, changed, or upgraded. He had to ask for at least one family member to travel with him as a chaperone and to stand in for his family at the wedding.

At that time, the trip between the two cities took four days by coach. Like all coach trips, there were stops on the way for various reasons including overnight stops at very primitive inns (*khans*). They provided no indoor toilet or bath facilities and very limited private sleeping facilities. They were dusty, often dirty and unsafe.

My parents were married in the Catholic church in Aleppo in 1926. My father convinced his niece Albera, at that time a single woman, to accompany him. She represented the Bazzoui family at the wedding. I was told the wedding was a great event.

However, my mother, upon her arrival to Baghdad, was disappointed in the primitive state of the city at that time. Baghdad's streets were narrow. The main roads were poorly paved. The buildings were not as well built as in Aleppo where fine stone was the standard. There were frequent dust storms that covered the city like a blanket, infiltrating windows and doors and driving thick red layers of dust into every nook and cranny in the home, necessitating days of rigorous cleaning. When it rained, on the other hand, the city roads turned into a muddy mess. Electricity was not available to every home and running water was only available to homes that had the necessary plumbing, which was not in every house.

In Baghdad, people did not take baths frequently. They had to rent a room in the public Turkish baths. The project of taking a bath in the public bath was an occasion that the women of the family enjoyed once a week. They would rent more than one room. They would take their towels, soaps, food, and their servants with them. The water would be steaming, and the baths were nice and warm. Little children of both sexes up to the age of three went with the women. After that the men took the boys with them to take a bath.

In Aleppo, on the other hand, things were much more civilized. Their homes were built of stone. Each house had a reservoir usually under the house where rain water was collected and used for cooking, bathing and even drinking in homes where the reservoirs were regularly and scrupulously cleaned. The streets were paved with cobblestones. The weather was more clement, and dust storms were not known there. It took my mother several years to adjust to her new life in Baghdad.

# The Man from Baghdad

My mother's genealogy is very interesting. Her great-great-great-grandfather came originally from Homs, a small town situated south of Aleppo. The city became well known recently due to the recent insurgence in Syria. In the 1770s, he migrated to Aleppo in search of work. He came with references as a master craftsman. He married a girl from a well-known family and started the tribe of the Homseys.

The history of Syria is replete with various nations passing through for trade or conquest. Alexander the Great passed through about 330 B.C., the Romans showed up around the time of Christ. The Crusaders passed through in several hordes, starting from the beginning of the second millennium. These Europeans and others, likely from countries nearby bordering the Mediterranean Sea, possibly Greece or Italy, mingled, married and cohabited with local girls over a period of several centuries leaving their genes, good and not so good, behind.

My mother's beauty was a result of this genetic heritage which sadly included thalassemia minor, which is Mediterranean anemia. I inherited this condition from her, and my daughter, Ban, also has it. We obviously have some vestiges of European genes in addition to the Chaldean and Arab genes. So much for my pure Arabic genealogy!

A few years later, when I was five, I took a trip with my mother back to Aleppo to visit my grandfather who was terminally ill. I was distressed at the squalor and the lack of security of the khans, and even at such a young age, I felt sorry for my mother to have had to travel to her future home in Baghdad under those circumstances.

My mother's father had worked as a businessman. His office was in an ancient and exotic bazaar. His two younger sons, George and Shafeeq, inherited his business and kept it until their death in the 1950s. His oldest son Joseph was a bank manager. He died in his fifties of a heart attack. My mother's younger sister Olga was married to a bank manager by the name of Gabriel Asswad. She had three daughters, Marie Jeanne, Claude, (who died in her early twenties in a car accident in Lebanon) and Josette. The youngest of my mother's sisters was Rose, never married, who died in her nineties several years ago.

My father and mother were blessed with five children. The oldest was Lydia. Unfortunately, she died at the age of two of meningitis. Her death was a tragedy for our immediate family as well as the rest of our extended family. Everyone loved her for her beauty, intelligence, and good nature. Mother was so attached to her that she lost her bearings and began her long slide into nervousness and chronic worry. As I was the second child, who became the oldest child by default, I was the beneficiary of my mother's fears, worries and therefore over-protectiveness.

Farouq, my younger brother, was born two years after me. Following that there was a period of five years when my mother had no births. Years later I learnt that she'd had two miscarriages during those years due to her psychological state. In 1936, my sister Nadia was born. Nadia was a challenge to our parents. She was fearful, colicky and cried constantly. She needed unceasing attention. We could never leave her at home with anybody but my mother. Nadia's own suffering became more apparent as she grew older. Our sister Ameera, the youngest sibling, was born in February 1941 when Iraq was at war with England. She was the most loving and loveable of all of us. She was our memory bank and our historian.

My mother was a kind and generous woman, though very emotional; she cried more easily than most and laughed heartily. She was famous for her cooking. She was a worrier and inclined toward depressive tendencies. She also suffered from palpitations that caused her to be constantly afraid of dying suddenly when her children were too young.

My father worked as the director of accounting in the ministry of finance. He took care of my mother and encouraged her, taking her to the best specialists in Iraq at that time. I remember in 1938, a medical specialist who had left Austria before Hitler took over, ended up in Baghdad as a refugee. He was gaining a good reputation in Iraq. Through friends my father asked him to see my mother. He came and examined her very thoroughly and told her that she was in good health and that she did not have a heart disorder. He recommended, as was the trend of that time that she take a trip for rest and recuperation. That year my father took a month of vacation from his government job and took all of us to Lebanon. That month of rest in the mountains helped my mother significantly but did not quite cure her. It is noteworthy to mention that that trip was the only vacation the Bazzoui family ever took together while I was growing up.

Our life in Baghdad, when my siblings and I were young, was a peaceful one, and our childhood was happy.

Our father used to tell my brother and me a chapter of his extraordinary adventures every night before going to sleep. We as children, for many years, heard the details of his travels in these foreign lands.

I remember Dad as a tall, well-built man, with black hair and a small mustache above the upper lip, the type of moustache which was the fashion among his peers. He was described by many of our friends as being handsome and debonair. Women who were close to our family thought that he was charming.

As a father he was serious, thoughtful, and kind. He tried his best to be a good example to us. He encouraged us to work hard and rewarded us when we excelled. When each of us reached three years old, he took the responsibility of our hygiene and manners from my mother. He gave my brother and me our biweekly baths, taught us how to dress, and how to use cutlery, he played table games with us, and helped us with our homework. When my sisters came along, my mother did the same for them.

Dad used to be perpetually serious as if he was always thinking about something. He did not talk very much, but when he did, we all listened. Mom was more light-hearted; she liked to joke and laugh. When she laughed, everything in the home brightened up and even Dad smiled. When she laughed, she'd start shaking and her whole body shook. We laughed at her laughter, and because we were happy, she was happy.

My parents lived a quiet, harmonious life. I never heard them argue. My father handled the money, being experienced in accounting through his job. They both discussed what they needed or what the children needed and how the money should be spent.

There was not much money. My mother often asked my father, "How are we going to manage?" Each time he answered, "God will provide." I always felt that she wasn't pleased with his answer and neither was he, but they did not discuss the matter further in our presence.

I don't remember using hand-me-downs, because my brother was rounder than me. The same was true with my sisters. Around the age of eight or nine, my father took my brother and me to the tailor on Rasheed Street who made our clothes. We were allowed one new suit a year and we usually got it just before Christmas. He chose the fabric, after having discussed the subject at length with my mother as far as style and color were concerned. Two weeks later we'd return to the tailor shop for a *prova*.

The *prova* was when the tailor checked how the suits fit us. Two weeks later we would pick up the suits. Then we had to stand for our mother's dreaded inspection and wait for her verdict on how she thought the suits fit us. On one occasion my dad had to take my suit back for alterations. Embarrassed, I had to wear last year's suit which was too tight and too short while waiting for the adjustment. To this day, I don't return things; no matter how ill-fitting, defective or unusable.

I had a lot of respect and love for my dad. A father's position in the Arabic family was the ruling head and his position and authority were never questioned. My father's position in the family was always clear to us even though he was a rather quiet man. In the same way, all members of the Bazzoui family revered him and looked up to him for advice and support.

Unfortunately, in 1941 Rashīd ʿAlī al-Gaylānī became the prime minister of Iraq, and he had some Nazi leanings. He declared war on England, which at that time was using the privileges of colonialism by utilizing Iraq's airports and army installations to fight the German interests in the Middle East. The current ruler of Iraq, ʿAbd al-Ilāh, his family and his cabinet fled the country, being considered British puppets. Of course, we were no match for Great Britain and the aid that was promised by the Reich did not arrive on time.

After a few days of skirmishes and a number of air raids by the British, Iraq surrendered, and the prime minister fled to the country. The worst thing that happened during these few days was the breakdown of law and order. This gave hoodlums opportunity to declare open season on people in general, and Jews in particular. There were lootings, rapes, murders, and other atrocities. That part of the Iraqi army that remained loyal to the king entered Baghdad and quelled the disorder and invited King ʿAbd al-Ilāh back.

Iraq during our teen years until 1958, however, was a wonderful place to live. The kingdom resumed its formalities, and while King Faisal II was too young to rule until 1953, his maternal uncle ʿAbd al-Ilāh acted as regent. British control and covert manipulation of the successive governments when there were moments of political tensions were well hidden from public discourse. The people of all sects and religions were hard working, interested in their families, and constantly striving to improve their lot. There was a culture of tolerance between the religions, but not equality. We all knew where we stood on the ladder of power. We were aware that there were many religions, sects, and languages, in our small world, but we managed to gloss over these differences and to live with them. Except for the looting, rapes and murders in 1941, there were, for all intents and purposes, no sectarian hostilities or brutalities.

I remember when I was growing up until I left Iraq how my Muslim friends used to talk about the pain, the thirst and the hunger their parents experienced in fulfilling their religious duty of fasting during daylight hours for the month of Ramadhan.

In the summer it was daylight from five a.m. until nine p.m., and the temperature stayed around 120° F between the hours of eleven a.m. until four in the afternoon. That required a lot of sacrifice—and dedication. We used to think that Christians got away easily by not eating meat two days a week.

As my friends grew to adulthood, they began to face the same penance as their parents. Those who couldn't fast due to medical reasons had to pay money to feed the needy. Some people closed their shops or took time off their work to fast. For those who fasted and their children, the happiest time of the year was when the Ramadhan month ended. It was followed by four days of feasting and celebrations. That's when we saw our friends having parties, wearing new clothes, riding in their cars and celebrating by singing together.

The feast was celebrated by the Muslims, though all other religions were given the days off too. (Although the Muslims worked during the high holy days of the Christians and Jews, the Christians and Jews were granted time off for their own high holy days, as well as the Muslim holy days without question.)

At one time I was very religious and used to read a lot of religious books, Christian and Muslim. I was very curious and eager to learn. Later on, as I grew older, I began to question some of the writings and the stories. I had a period when I was very worried about the believability of the Holy Books. At one time I was so depressed because of losing my faith in the books that I thought life was not worth living. I talked to my father about it. He did not have answers for me, maybe because he had the same ideas I had. I did not want to talk to my Jesuit teachers, even though I respected them, because I thought they were set in their faith and would not be impartial with my concerns. Fortunately, that period passed and I developed my own beliefs and understanding of life and death.

In the 1950s and 1960s we noticed more distance and strain between the various religions and sects. We were more conscious of the differences, and more circumspect in addressing each other. The Jewish community began to withdraw from social contact. My friends stopped coming out to congregate by my house where we as thirteen- and fourteen-year-olds used to get together to chat, ride our bicycles, or even play marbles. Our Jewish neighbors who lived next door, used to rely on me to switch on the lights or turn on the stove on the Sabbath, stopped asking me to do so, even when I offered.

Our family had many Jewish friends in our neighborhood, in school, and at work. My parents knew more of what was going on than we kids knew, but they did not discuss any of the problems with us. Gradually, many of these friends started to leave Iraq: selling their homes and their businesses. I was in medical school when all these changes began to happen. There were seven Jewish students with me in class. Around that time, or perhaps a few years earlier, we read in the newspapers that the government had uncovered a communist cell in Baghdad that was conspiring to overthrow the royal government and establish a communist state in Iraq. Four men were hanged after a thorough investigation. All four were Jewish. That created an atmosphere of paranoia in various sectors of society. In 1948, with the establishment of the state of Israel, speculation about the presence of Jews in Iraq began to surface.

In 1950, a number of explosions in Baghdad scared the population immensely as Baghdad had been a peaceful city not known for such terrorist acts. These explosions occurred in front of, or very close to, several synagogues. There were no known casualties, but the Jewish community took these incidents as threats from the Muslim community—or even the government. Many years later, we learned that they were perpetrated by one of the Zionist terrorist organizations, such as the Irgun or the Haganah. They were calculated to scare the Jewish community, increase their feelings of insecurity, and entice them to migrate to the new Jewish state.

By the end of 1951 or thereabout, the overwhelming majority of the Iraqi Jews had already left Iraq, most of them immigrating to Israel. It was never the same after that. They left a deep gap in business, culture, arts, as well as in our lives in Iraq. They had lived in our country since Nebuchadnezzar, the Assyrian emperor, who had conquered their land in Palestine during two wars, (597 B.C.), and brought them as exiles to Babylon. A few professional and religious Jews stayed a while longer. For a very long time after their departure, life remained sad, desolate, and uncertain for the other minorities. The seven Jewish students in my medical school class all left in one day; even though they were within a year of graduation.

I was told when I was growing up that our ancestors on my father's side were inhabitants of this part of the world for at least two thousand years. The Bazzoui family came originally from the north of Iraq, probably as the descendants of the Chaldean empire that ruled Mesopotamia, parts of Turkey, Persia and Syria. Some of the inhabitants of Iraq at this time still speak the Chaldean language which is similar to the ancient language. My ancestors converted to Christianity when Saint Thomas passed through this land on his way to Persia and India. Muslim armies conquered and ruled Iraq around 633-634 A.D. As Christians, we were given the chance to remain Christians if we paid the *jizya* (tax).

I was told by my father that many of my forebears were very well educated in whatever field of knowledge was known at that time, such as math, languages, religion and history. In fact, my father's paternal uncle was promoted to the highest position, patriarch in the Chaldean Catholic Church, the eastern branch of Catholic church. A patriarch was selected by the Pope to govern the Chaldean Catholic Church. Father told me that in addition to his knowledge in theology and dogma, he spoke, wrote, and read seven languages. Languages helped Christians find jobs in ancient times. Not only did they act as interpreters for the rulers, but they excelled in translating Greek, Latin and Persian to Arabic and vice versa. They were also doctors for the caliphs and even viziers. My father's maternal uncle, Cardinal Tappoonie, was the first cardinal selected by the pope in the Arabic-speaking countries.

My father used to talk from time to time about the history of Christians in Iraq as told to him by his family. Iraq, before the arrival of Islam, was mostly Christian and to a lesser degree Jewish with some minorities such as the Zoroastrians, and pagans. As a matter of fact, even now there are ancient churches, convents, and other religious edifices scattered all over Iraq, especially in the north, in addition to the more modern places of worship. The Islamic conquest of Iraq followed by the occupation of Syria and Palestine brought with it a frightening change in the lives of the Christians and Jews of these nations. The choices they were given were unbelievably disturbing. Iraqis either converted to Islam, paid the *jizya*, or were killed.

Many of the Christians were poor people at that time. To them, converting was the least destructive choice. Many of them rejected these choices out of religious fervor and were put to the sword. Some went underground and survived. Although many, who were educated and had knowledge in certain fields such as medicine, languages, and science, were spared and given distinguished jobs in the service of the rulers.

History books relate the varying attitudes of the caliphs toward the Christians. These attitudes wavered from mass persecution and killings to freedom to practice their religion without constraint. These choices and the subsequent changes in the attitude of the rulers left the minorities with perpetual anxiety and uncertainty about their fate. The same attitude existed until the time I left Iraq and is one that remains to this day. What is happening to the Christians in Iraq today is a more drastic repetition of the historical scene over the centuries.

The overwhelming state of mind among all non-Muslim minorities in Iraq, and perhaps in all Islamic countries, is the perennial fear for their future. Over the years this has led to accepting a place in society as a second-class citizen, when it comes to the acquisition of high-ranking jobs in the government, in business, and in institutions of knowledge. Fear of reprisals in asking for equal rights has led to a feeling of hopelessness in aspiring for positions of importance in the above fields despite the acknowledged presence of competence or even excellence in these fields. Hence, they turned to private enterprise to hack out a living in a place where they and their forefathers had lived for a millennium and a half.

Migration has been a way out of this impasse. After each period of tyranny and persecution, large numbers of families and individuals find their way to other countries. Even if the three choices given to the Christians were not practiced since the early part of the twentieth century, the feeling that we as "infidels" were not wanted was pervasive at least in our subconscious. At one time, the number of Christians in Iraq approximated two million. I have read the number is now three hundred thousand or less and constantly decreasing.

Our male ancestors wore the same outfits as the tribal men wear today. They wore long shirts that fell to the ground, with a fabric belt tied around the waist. The color was either white or off white. For a headdress they used a large white kerchief occasionally speckled with a black pattern tied around the head. Some form of jacket completed their costume. The headdress is significant in so much as the color and patterns depict the status and tribe of the wearer.

More recently, men have begun to wear western clothes especially after the country was split from the Ottoman Empire. My father and all his contemporaries wore elegant western clothing as a rule, depending on their financial abilities.

Mary and Emile Bazzoui on the day
of their wedding in 1926, and in 1928.

## Chapter Two

# Growing Up in Baghdad

In general, as I look back at my family, I remember very few serious conflicts, arguments, or fights. We were really close, and we had a lot of affection for each other. Our parents were equally loving and protective. My brother Farouq and I were especially close. He not only respected me and my opinions, but genuinely cared for me as I did for him. I was blessed to have a tightly knit middle-class family.

My father provided us with a comfortable life. We had everything we needed to survive. The political system was stable until 1958, and the only complaint most people had were the sandstorms that caused havoc with breathing. That and the problem of cleaning seemed to be the most common topics of conversation. Dry weather was also a serious problem, though. Gardeners had to water everything they grew, but thanks to the Tigris River, we had ample amounts of water to remedy that. Our plants and trees never showed the healthy green color we later grew accustomed to in Pennsylvania. The most difficult problem was the heat. We took siestas for about two hours after lunch. People closed their shops, restaurants and offices, and some opened again from four until eight p.m. And it wasn't uncommon for those who had basements in their homes to stay there for the hottest hours of the day.

The seasons in Iraq are dominated by a very short spring which merges within two or three weeks into a long, hot summer that can be very debilitating. Summer stretches from the end of April to the end of October. The temperature can reach 120 degrees Fahrenheit, making it even more difficult to work outside, or even inside, because of the destructive heat.

There was no air conditioning in Iraq when I was growing up. We had table and ceiling fans. There was a contraption to help with the heat, consisting of a large wooden cubic frame covered by a blanket of straw placed in an open window, with a constant stream of water drops spread over the straw. It is difficult to describe better than this. When a fan was directed at it, a cool refreshing breeze was generated. That helped during the very hot and dry hours of the day.

At night, Iraqis slept on the flat roofs of their houses. There were no peaked roofs in Iraq. At about six in the evening, the ladies of the house or their servants would go to the roof, unfold the summer mattresses which were stored in attic-like-closets on the roofs. Then they made the beds and set up the mosquito nets. By nine or ten at night, the beds were cool and comfortable. We woke early as the sun also rose early on summer days and could be monstrous.

# The Man from Baghdad

Of course, as the whole family slept on the roof, far from the street below, they had to be concerned with potential robbers. It happened to us once. I went to my bedroom before sunrise and found it plundered and then checked my parent's bedroom which was also torn asunder. I quickly ran to the roof to tell my father. We went downstairs and found the whole house had been ransacked by robbers while we slept. Our doors had been securely locked but those thieves must have been adept at picking locks. None of our stolen goods were ever recovered.

When Dad worked for the government, he made about the equivalent of fifty to sixty dollars a month. For the thirties this was a little above the average income for a middle-class family in Iraq. We lived in a rented house with two bedrooms and no electricity. Every evening my father would light up some oil lamps hung on different walls to light our living areas. In 1933 my father bought a small piece of land outside town which was very cheap, and he built a house. It had an Arabic design which took into consideration the terrible heat in the summer. The house had a large living room that opened into three bedrooms, a dining room, a bathroom and at the rear of the living room it opened into a courtyard, a kitchen, and a large cellar that was about four steps down where we spent the hot summer afternoon hours.

The house was in an isolated area and my father's family was worried about our safety. It was a beautiful house and many people soon started to build close to us. By then it was 1937, my father's job had improved, and there were three children in our family. The house also had a garage but, of course, we didn't have a car. We rented it to a man who did ironing of clothes for people, using a charcoal for his irons. He had to constantly light the charcoal. I used to hang out with him sometimes, watching how he ironed for the men in the neighborhood. He had a thriving business. By then my grandfather had passed away. He had lived with us for one or two years. He had been the postmaster in Basra. He must have been in his 70s, he seemed very old to us. We were afraid of him because he used a cane which he sometimes banged on the floor when my brother and I were naughty. When we behaved and listened, he told us stories. We loved that. My sister, Nadia, was about one year old when we moved to the new house.

The police station was about a half mile away. We had Polus, a 30ish married Christian male servant from the north of Iraq who lived with us and helped with the cleaning, and cooking, etc. Polus walked my brother and me to school in the morning and back in the afternoon. He visited his family once or twice a week for overnight visits. His wife and children visited us often too.

It is interesting to mention that this man whom we loved and respected worked for our family for about twenty years and when his four boys graduated from high school, he asked to leave. It was a sad day when he left, but he introduced his mother-in-law as a replacement. Martha was in her late 50s and was a good and loving woman who was taught to cook Syrian foods by my mother, and even became famous for her cooking. She died in her 70s after my mother died. She took care of our family as her own until her death.

# The Man from Baghdad

One evening in 1995, the telephone rang, a faint voice of an old man asked if I was Widad Effendi. (Effendi is an old Turkish word that means Mr., used in Arabic to address a gentleman.) I was confused and shocked, having not heard that in many years. I told him I was Widad, the voice said, "I am Polus."

We both started crying.

He told me his sons had all immigrated to the USA after high school and were all citizens of the USA now. His sons had managed to bring their parents to the USA recently. He told me with great pride that all four of his sons graduated from college in the US, two are lawyers, all are successful. He thanked me and my deceased parents for all we did for his family. His wife came on the phone and told me the same. That, for me, was a magnificent phone call. It took me a long time to bring my memories and my emotions under control.

Memories of my father are also impossible for me to forget. They keep recurring in my thoughts as if I am trying to discover how much of his guidance I passed on to my own children.

I remember him taking Farouq and me with him to the Old Baghdad Bazaar every month when I was six years old through eleven or so. The open-air market was filled with exotic spices, fruits, meats … almost anything a person could need. Smells drifted out to the street from the huge array of spice bins. It was a crowded, busy place filled with people, as well as animals. Donkeys, mules, sheep, and chickens intermingled with shoppers.

We had to hold Dad's hands lest we get lost from him, for fear of *staying lost forever* in the huge bazaar. You could buy anything that is usable or edible in bulk, there was shop after shop of spices, cheeses and butter stands in crowded rows. Cooking oils, gee (lamb fat), rice, bulgers, teas and sugar were also displayed in bulk. In another area of the massive bazaar there were school items such as pads, pencils, pen inks. It was literally a wonderland.

When Dad finished the shopping, he hired a man with a mule to load everything on his mule and take the spoils of our shopping to our home. My mother would be waiting. The mule man carried everything into the kitchen and put the bags where she asked him. Meanwhile Dad took Farouq and me to a kabob restaurant for lunch. Such treasured memories.

Usually Dad came home from work at about 1:30 in the afternoon. Dad ate lunch and then took a siesta for an hour or two after that. My dad did not return to work after his siesta and he spent his time with us and our mother. He had a few friends and neighbors who sometimes dropped by and he often visited his brother or his friends.

Occasionally, he took Farouq and me with him to his favorite tea shop. Teas shops in Iraq were similar to coffee shops in the west without the food. They served only one kind of tea and the *nargeela*, which is a kind of Asian smoking contraption that runs inhaled cigarette smoke through water to reduce its impact. When a client feels like it, he orders one and it would be prepared for him to use for the evening.

For my brother and me, these jaunts to the tea shop were memorable events. They taught us to play backgammon which, before the advent of dominoes, was the most popular game for "grown up" men, and it gave us a feeling of importance. The conversations that were exchanged introduced us to business talk, political discussions, and historical stories that my father and his friends exchanged while playing backgammon and drinking tea after tea. Mother was relieved to see us go and pleased to see us return.

Saturday evenings, when Farouq and I were four and six years old, we had to take our baths as men without my mother being there. My father showed us how to use the *leefa*, (an organic sponge), and how to use soap. The reward for our endeavor after we dried, dressed and combed our hair was special tea and ham sandwiches for our dinner. (At that time there was no ham in Iraq for religious reasons. But on Saturdays, small quantities of ham arrived from Lebanon for the Christian families.) And we each got a paper-thin sandwich of that delicacy as a reward.

Once or twice a year the government gave a ball for high-ranking government officials at the municipal building. This was a very special ball, attended by the prime minister, during the years 1936-1938. My father wore his tuxedo and my mom wore beautiful evening gowns. They strutted around for us while we lay on the floor on our bellies with our hands holding our heads as we admired the show. To us they were the most glamorous and beautiful couple in the world. Then they would leave in a horse-drawn carriage.

Another ritual Dad taught Farouq and me, was the proper care and cleaning of Persian carpets. At the end of winter, all carpets were removed, and the tile floors cleaned to prepare for the long summer. A special group of strong men did this service. They took the carpets out of the house to the driveway or veranda where they shook them up and down until all the dust accumulated over the winter was gone. Then they swept the rugs, rolled them or folded them into bales and wrapped them with a special covering. They were taken to the storage room at the back of our house, stored for the summer, until it was time to return them to the tile floors the next winter. The day this operation takes place is important for the children to help supervise because these rugs were considered a treasure and an asset to the family. They needed to be carefully accounted for. My dad felt it important that we learned to be responsible for what we owned. Some of these rugs were taken to the river bank, washed, cleaned, and returned to us after they dried.

Another social activity was a Syrian tradition that came from the French. I remember the first Thursday of each month was our family's Open House Day. Our family received their friends in an unofficial way in their homes and it became known as the Bazzoui salon. We offered small cookies, baklava, and tea, and in the summer, cold drinks. Some played cards, some listened to music, others chatted in small groups, and some even danced. We, meaning my siblings and me, served and socialized with the guests. We felt important, and it improved our self-confidence and socialization skills. I don't remember when it stopped, most likely when my mother became ill at the age of fifty-two.

Despite our lively social lives, we lived modestly, and my parents had to save as much money as they could. We did not have a car until 1956. We did not have a television until a few years later. At that time a servant was customary. The cost was no more than one dinar a month, (equivalent of three dollars and sixty cents at the time.) We provided a place for the servant to sleep and keep their belongings; we also fed them and provided clothing with our hand-me-downs. The servants also had one day off per week to spend with their family.

My father had also trained as an accountant and was given a job in the Ministry of Finance. He kept this job for thirty years. However, at age sixty-two my father became the accounts director of the Royal Iraqi Spinning and Weaving Company, which was a prestigious position. We insisted he employ a chauffeur to take him back and forth to work. He accepted it because he was having problems with his vision. Every day or two, he asked his chauffeur to stop by the fruit market to buy whatever the owner recommended. They were the only items he shopped for, outside the trips to the bazaar. All of the daily shopping was done by Martha in the early morning.

Growing up, one of my most frightening memories was when my father was diagnosed with pneumonia. I must have been about thirteen. We were not told what was wrong, but I knew that he was seriously ill because my mother was crying all the time. There was no penicillin then. Fortunately, our doctor found some sulfadiazine which he prescribed for my father. Dad began to show improvement the following day. It is hard to describe the terror that I experienced when I feared losing my father. He was like the sheikh of our family.

Medical care was not easily available by doctors in the Thirties. Doctors made house calls. One treatment that was very popular was "cupping"—placing a small burning piece of cotton in a small thin glass cup and applying it to the back where it sucks the air and attaches to the skin until the little fire dies out. I cannot describe it more adequately, but it was used for colds. Another favorite "remedy" was castor oil. It was very nasty-tasting drug that tormented my childhood. For lack of any other medical treatment, castor oil was prescribed regularly, almost bimonthly, by our doctor. My father used to bribe me with a coin for every spoonful of that monstrous medicine I'd swallow. Doctor's orders.

Dad was always low-keyed and patient. He did not have any hobbies besides his children and our interests. He smoked every day, but only drank on rare occasions. He did not indulge himself in any way. Well, except for those daily shaves with a straight blade razor from his faithful barber, Mustafa. I remember Mustafa, who also cut our hair as we grew up, knocking at the door every morning at seven to shave my father. Dad always had his own shaving paraphernalia ready. I was told that that was the routine for all the Christian men in our neighborhood. I remember Mustafa crying when my father died, having shaved him six days a week for forty years, including the morning before he died.

# The Man from Baghdad

My brother and I went to a private primary school, (Madame Adil's), a Lebanese teacher who educated half of the Iraqi leader's children of that time. After that, we went to the American Jesuit High School which was the best high school in Iraq. It competed with the Jewish Alliance High School. My two sisters went to the French Nun School for their primary and secondary education; both of them spoke, read, and wrote French, English and Arabic.

Unfortunately, as Dad's expenses swelled with four children, their schools, and my mother's poor health; he could not continue to pay the annual mortgage payments. He owed about nine hundred dollars. The only unusual expense we had was a servant to help my mother with cleaning and cooking and to walk us kids to school and back. It appeared to my father at the time that the bank did not want to extend the mortgage because someone the bank manager was close to wanted the house and was willing to pay the bank a good profit. My father was forced to sell the house, which by then was on a very desirable location. With what he got for the house, he bought a new piece of land in a new expanding development. He proceeded to build our second house, which was more up-to-date and larger with two floors in design.

By this time, we were two teenage boys and two girls, ages seven and two. We needed three bedrooms on the second floor with two bathrooms and a half bathroom with living room, dining room, and a kitchen downstairs. We moved to that house in 1943. It was a beautiful house on a corner lot along two modern wide boulevards. It became the gathering place for all the kids in our neighborhood who were our age. We had Antar, our German shepherd, bicycles, a radio and even a telephone. There were no televisions yet.

By then my brother and I were in the Jesuit high school. We were picked up in the morning by the school bus, which, by the way, looked exactly like the American school buses of today. Our school hours were from eight till four. We were loaded with home-work every day, six days a week. When I see today's parents fighting against home-work for their kids because the "kids have a right to enjoy their childhood," I don't understand what they mean.

We were children who studied hard, played hard, and socialized. We and our friends were happy children, even with our long hours and our homework. All the schools in Iraq had the same hours. They all sent children home with homework, some more than others. Ours and the Alliance (the Jewish high school) had the most. We participated athletically in baseball, boxing, volleyball, soccer, basketball and outdoor handball courts. We had two fifteen-minute breaks around ten and two. We also had a half hour for lunch. Farouq and I felt for a long time that high school was the most rewarding and wonderful time in our lives. There was great stress on languages, meaning Arabic and English. Math came next. We took geometry, solid geometry, algebra and trigonometry. Some of us took calculus on the side. I graduated in 1946. My brother graduated in 1948.

The Jesuit fathers who were American from the New England Diocese offered to send me to the USA on a full scholarship, to attend Boston College to study mechanical engineering. I was 16 and I was very excited. However, my parents said, "No! You are too young." They worried about the distance and the difficulty to travel in case of an emergency.

Through the years, my father taught my brother and me how to take care of our future families and my sisters what to expect from their future husbands when they married. Of course, I can say the same about my mother's influence on all of us. She worked with the servant to take care of the house. She sewed my sister's clothes. She taught them to pray, how to behave in public, and the accepted etiquette of those days. Looking back at my family of origin, I feel fortunate and grateful to have had them.

Perhaps we were lucky to have grown up without a television or a car. We did not miss what we had never had.

Widad with his parents in 1930 on the left, and Widad and Farouq with Mary and Emile Bazzoui in 1933.

The Bazzoui family in 1940:
daughters Nadia and Ameera in the front row; Widad,
mother Mary, father Emile, with Farouq in the back row.

The Bazzoui home in Baghdad.

# Chapter Three

# Medical School and the Army

Iraq, until the time I graduated high school, offered free education to all citizens and residents who were eligible and interested, from grade school through high school. That's why at the time of the US invasion in 2003 it was estimated that Iraq had 97% literacy, the highest in the Middle East and many other places, even Europe. High-school graduates who obtained a certain minimum average on the national test were eligible to attend free public colleges. The quality of the offered education varied, like elsewhere in the world, depending on students' background and motivation, as well as teachers' interest and expertise, and other factors. Private high schools, on the other hand, usually had motivated students from educated and financially comfortable families; and were not free. I can easily say that Baghdad College High School run by the Jesuit priests graduated the majority of Iraqi leaders in finance, politics, and education of my generation. Our graduates went to universities all over the world. I obtained a high grade in my national tests. I'd long been intrigued with math and design, and initially had a strong desire to study engineering. At that time Iraq offered only civil engineering, but I was not interested in that.

My mother had always dreamed that one of her sons would become a doctor. Being the older of the two boys, I took the plunge. I had no problem getting admitted to medical school based on my grades and on the quota of slots in the school given by the government to Christians. There were a similar number of openings for Jews. My brother eventually went to the engineering school.

The medical school was fashioned after the English system of education; it was for six years in succession. It was my luck that the faculty that year decided to add a preparatory year to help students catch up who were not knowledgeable in English or chemistry.

Medical school was long and demanding; fortunately, it was more interesting and fulfilling than I expected. My medical class cohorts were a collection of young, enthusiastic, and hardworking students. About one third of the class were women. They came from all parts of Iraq. Ten male students were Christian, seven were Jewish, and the other two hundred twenty-three students were Muslim.

It is hard to understand the hostilities and wars between religions today because they stand in such contrast to the good relations we experienced then. What we encountered in medical school was mutual respect and lasting friendship. We were almost unaware of the religions of the kids sitting beside us while working on the same projects. A certain respect and interdependence were the prevailing feelings for each other. I remember every evening we used to gather about seven of us in my home to study. Coffee with some sandwiches was prepared by my mom before she went to bed. We usually studied until one o'clock when my friends headed home. And those friendships have lasted until now. Of course, death has reduced our numbers in the last few years. But at that time, religions stayed at home and were not in the streets as it is today.

The medical school lessons were in English. Those of us who graduated from Baghdad College were fluent in English unlike graduates from public schools who needed our help with translations, etc. We worked together to achieve our goals.

After seven hard years my peers and I graduated and were given our diplomas as Bachelor of Medicine and Surgery. Our joy in graduation did not last long. We were immediately conscripted in the reserve army to serve for eighteen months. The first three months were for training in warfare, the use of weapons and even horseback riding that was, at that time, considered important in case there was a need to reach casualties in mountainous areas. In addition, we were given lectures about war injuries and military hospital management as well as the responsibility for the training of our medical assistants.

That period of training was very exciting and vigorous. We enjoyed the strenuous athletic training. The three months proved to be a bonding exercise that brought all the young men even closer to each other. Following the three-month training, we were appointed to various military hospitals to work and we lived in the barracks. We were given the rank of captain in the Army Medical Corps, as well as a heavy revolver to carry when we were in parades. Of course, we all trained to fire the weapon in case we needed to use it.

The women who graduated with us did not have to join the army but were sent to various internship programs in big hospitals around the country ahead of the men.

It was around that time, while a junior in high school that Nadia took her first overdose; even though that act was seen as a gesture, it was something new in our social circle. As I mentioned earlier, Nadia was always a withdrawn, rather reticent girl who kept her thoughts and feelings to herself, thus leaving her family who wanted to share their lives with her very frustrated. When Mom attempted to reach out to her, she was consistently rebuffed with anger. Nadia was in high school and was continuing to have problems with isolation and angry outbursts against Mom. Because of not having experienced this kind of emergency in our lives we listened to our family doctor who was also a friend of the family and had known about Nadia's problems. He suggested that Nadia might be more comfortable if she stayed away from her mother. Dad and Mom decided to send her to a nun's boarding school in Aleppo for one year. She was to stay with one of my aunts on weekends and vacations and spend time with her cousins there. My father was by then alarmed at what was happening to Nadia and to the rest of the family. He reluctantly agreed to the idea of sending her to her aunt.

# The Man from Baghdad

Nadia did not write a single word to Mom and Dad during that year until school ended and she was ready to come home. It became clear to me later that she harbored deep-rooted anger and possibly hate for my parents and possibly her siblings for unknown reasons that she must have imagined, possibly due to paranoid thinking. I knew for sure that my parents loved her and respected her as well if not more than they did the rest of us. We siblings tiptoed around her and remained baffled by what we saw.

But back to my military duties, I served in the army during a time of peace in Iraq. We still had our duties as physicians to take care of the soldiers and their families, if they lived close to the camp. It was in that role as the assistant to the commanding physician that I experienced my first medical emergency. It was an epidemic of meningococcal meningitis. It started insidiously with one case in a soldier who went on leave to his family one weekend and came back with high fever and severe headache. When I examined him, I noted that he was obtunded and a very sickly-looking young man. He told me that one of his children had the same symptoms.

On examination, I found that he was clammy, feverish, and rather clouded in sensorium. In lying supinely, I found on trying to bend his neck forward that his neck was rigid and unbendable, a condition we call opisthotonus. This sign is one of three classic signs of meningitis. I did a lumbar puncture, spinal tap, and found the spinal fluid was turbid which indicated that he had a bacterial kind of infection involving the meninges, (the covering of the brain).

I gave him an intravenous injection of Sulfadiazine and isolated him from his platoon.

Meningitis is caused mostly by a bacterium called Neisseria meningitidis. In older people it can be caused by streptococcus pneumonia. It is spread by breathing or coughing in closed areas. Sulfadiazine at that time was the drug of choice. It was given intravenously or by mouth.

After that first patient, we were flooded not only by the military, but by their families. Some of them were treated by us in our small hospital and some who appeared to be too sick we sent to our "Walter Reed" in Baghdad. We had one hundred and four cases in all before we could control the situation. There were three mortalities. That was my first serious medical crisis without supervision by a superior. It gave me a feeling of confidence and elation in my new career. Apart from that very interesting experience, the year and a half of my military service passed with no adventures. The barracks were about an hour and a half away from my family.

A friend of mine, Gilbert, shared a shack with me in the wilderness about fifteen minutes from the camp. The shack had a thatched roof. Night after night we went to bed with the sound of snakes slithering between the layers of the thatched roof. We wondered when they are going to fall on us when we were asleep, but that never happened. What did happen was meeting one of these abhorrent animals as I came home after work. It raised its head and watched as I pulled my gun and shot it hoping that I got it. Low and behold that miracle happened. I left the dead snake inside the door to give my roommate a little scare. It did. He never forgave me for that. From then on, we were always very vigilant about the noises in the ceiling of our shack.

It was during that year that central and southern Iraq suffered the worst flood in modern Iraq history. The government of Iraq over many decades had experienced historic floods usually starting with the Tigris, followed by the Euphrates River rising way above their banks and inundating farms, villages, and even cities. A flood in a country that prided itself on its agricultural products was not too much of a problem because of the enrichment of the soil that the rivers brought to the farmlands. However, when Baghdad, the capital, was threatened, the damage to roads, buildings, businesses and other facilities was not acceptable.

As I was growing up in Baghdad in the Forties and Fifties, a high and very long dyke had been built by the government to protect Baghdad. That dyke was on the eastern side of Baghdad extending from the area where the mighty Tigris courses through the city and ended a short distance after it exits the city.

During the flood of 1954, the dyke had to be breached before the river reached Baghdad, to allow the raging waters to escape out of the river into the desert outside Baghdad's east side. It was around March/April of that year that the flood water surrounding the city was so high that motorboats were needed to transport people in and out of Baghdad for several weeks. In those days, the Iraq government prepared the city when snow in the Ararat mountains of Turkey began to thaw. Unfortunately, today most of these waters have been dammed by the government of

Turkey in order to use the water there, depriving Iraq of desperately needed water.

One night during the peak of the deluge I was ordered to take my medical platoon with our ambulances and emergency equipment to Baghdad. The members of the team prepared their best uniforms to march the following morning in a military celebration parade. Because of the rumors of high waters around Baghdad, we decided to leave the ambulances behind and borrow what we needed from the Baghdad hospital in the morning. We were to be ready if we were needed medically during the parade.

We started to drive around 1900 hours, to be correct in military language. We drove southwest for a couple of hours unaware of the seriousness of the high waters outside the breached dyke. It was pitch dark at the makeshift 'port' when we arrived at the edge of the expanding waters. There was a state of utter confusion.

We had military orders to get to the capital for the parade, the farmers were bringing in their produce, and the travelers who left Baghdad in the morning for business were all fighting to get on small boats that had been rounded up for that purpose. Of course, we did not know how far we had to go to reach the dyke, or how safe it was. Because I was captain in rank with a platoon and I had my orders, my platoon and I managed to take over two larger boats and we waded in what was quickly becoming a muddy, slippery landing area to get to the boats.

By the time we embarked, we were wet up to our thighs. The horror of that night will never leave me as long as I live. The boats chugged along in very shallow waters at first, and then in deeper waters, and finally in raging waters with many dark figures popping in and out of the churning dark waters around us. Some of the passengers were seeing superstitious beings jumping at them from the waters. Some thought that they were seeing small islands jutting from the vast expanse of water that we were navigating in the dark. There were snakes, foxes, wolves, and deer struggling for their lives trying to jump into our boats.

My fellow companions started praying loudly. Some were screaming with fear. The women were hysterical. Some were just paralyzed with fear. Our two boats were old and rickety. They had one forward light. They heaved and creaked and rose with mounting waves and plunged to the depth causing even the heartiest amongst us to feel the end was nigh.

It was on that horrible night that I wished I had gone against my mother's wishes and learnt how to swim in the Tigris like some of my friends did. I wished that the army had taught us to swim instead of teaching us horseback riding. But then looking at that vast, heaving mass of dark water I knew that even the best swimmers would not have had a chance.

As we looked upon a small island as we passed, we knew that we were not alone in this terrible fate. Snakes, small critters, foxes and other animals had already found their way there; all hanging on for dear life on these small islets. We were better off than them. We realized that chugging in our boat held much more hope than being on those islands for an unknown period of time.

It was about one o'clock in the morning when we finally landed at the dyke. The military had sent a bus to pick us up. Exhausted, cold, wet and still shaky, I was given a ride to my parent's place and the rest of the team were taken to the barracks. My father opened the door not knowing that I was coming to Baghdad. He was shocked to see me. He did not even know that the dyke had broken late that afternoon. Being safely with my parents and siblings was the best treat for me that night.

Military service was obligatory for all men who graduate from any college in the land. In a way it was a way to pay the government for our free education. We really did not want it to end because of the challenges and the training we got. We were paid a small salary which was the only drawback. But after years of no financial rewards, we were eager to start earning our keep. During the last month of our service, we were called to Baghdad to the medical school to select the residency program where we were going to be appointed upon finishing our military service. We were discharged with the rank of captain and remained in the reserves. Two weeks later we started our residency.

The medical class of 1953 included only forty-four graduates. We started as one hundred twenty students in 1946. Then the medical faculty added another year when we were already in our second year. They admitted one hundred twenty-five more students to our class—bringing the total to two hundred and forty-five. The grueling classes, the failures, and the voluntary withdrawals were some of the reasons the number of graduates was so much lower than when we began. Seven Jewish students also decided to leave Iraq in 1951. Forty-four students were all that were left to finally graduate.

Since I was the highest-ranking graduate in medical school, I had the privilege to select the specialty of my choice. I chose internal medicine as my residency program. King Faisal II was unable at that time to attend our medical school graduation (which was the custom); he honored me by sending me an Omega watch as recognition of my work. A few years ago, I gave it to my daughter, Reem.

I was very lucky to spend over a year as a resident with Dr. William Hargreaves, the British professor in internal medicine who taught in India before he came to Iraq. We were the beneficiaries of the Indian Independence War when most of the high-ranking military doctors chose to leave that country and look for teaching jobs elsewhere. Professor Hargreaves was one of these doctors, and a remarkable teacher. His strength was in tropical diseases and cardiology. He believed in teaching students the art of medicine before learning diagnosis and treatment. He insisted that we diagnose conditions by the principles that the father of modern medicine, Dr. William Osler, taught. He was very intent in teaching good habits by first taking a thorough history followed by meticulous physical examination consisting of inspection, palpation, percussion and auscultation before we ever dare to ask for labs and X-rays.

This kind of stress on the physical examination, unfortunately understated now in medical schools, was what all graduates needed to learn before assuming responsibilities in the medical field. I was always grateful to him for insisting that I master the craft of medicine before learning the science part. Residents attended clinical lectures and seminars throughout the whole year. They learned how to do lab tests and how to present our findings to our teachers.

We were supposed to admit patients to the hospital from the outpatient department and from the emergency room. We started treatment ourselves unless they had a serious problem, at which time we sought the help of the senior resident. Residents did the preliminary exams and investigations and arrived at an initial diagnosis to start the treatment. In the morning when the professor arrived, every necessary piece of information, gleaned from the patient or family as well as the workup, was to be there. In addition to the admissions, we were responsible for the care of the patients who were already in the hospital.

I was also fortunate to train under Dr. Jack Abboodi, professor of neurology and psychiatry, during my neurology rotation. Dr. Abboodi was the father of psychiatry in Iraq; he inspired a host of medical students to pursue a career in neurology and or psychiatry.

A man of short stature who spoke softly and in the most modest way as he analyzed every case, Dr. Abboodi gave the differential diagnosis and the reasons for arriving at his conclusions in a most convincing way. His rounds were the most interesting of all the rounds in the teaching hospital.

Occasionally, my fellow residents were called to help in the emergency room when the doctor there needed help. I enjoyed being needed in the E.R. because it exposed me to a variety of urgent cases in various specialties that later on in my career were invaluable. Looking back at that period of my life I have to say, despite the long hours, the anxiety, the hard work and lack of sleep, it was the most exciting part of my medical education. It was not unusual to go to bed at two a.m. and start the next day at six a.m. day after day. That year passed very quickly, but at the end of that intense program, my colleagues and I were ready to face life in our various fields.

Dr. Widad Bazzoui 1953

## Chapter Four

# My First Medical Position

Because I graduated at the top of my class, I had another privilege. In addition to selecting my residency program, I was given the right to choose the place to practice after residency before any of my colleagues. We were obligated to pay the government back for the free medical education by serving five years in rural areas. I could not wait!

It was not a difficult task for me to make my choice. I had already cased the available rural areas where we were supposed to work. I chose a small town that straddled the Euphrates River where several years before the government had constructed a huge dam to regulate the water flow to the central agricultural part of Iraq. The region was a fertile, verdant land that produced a great variety of vegetables, fruits, grains, and an abundance of dates. The weather was very pleasant, and the people were eager to finally have a doctor on board.

In preparation for the arrival of medical care to that area, a small outpatient clinic and a good-sized house with three bedrooms, a bathroom, and modern kitchen were built for that area. I was to prepare the clinic with what I needed to provide care for the people, and to start my work as soon as I could. My job was to take care of the medical needs of adults and children and take care of all kinds of health problems. I was ready and eager.

The name of the place was Saddat al Hindiyah, translated to English it meant the Hindeyah Dam. Although the place was classified as rural, it had clean water, electricity, telephone service, and reasonable roads. I was very pleased with my choice. My work hours for the government were from seven to one, but after that I could do what I wished. So, as all Iraqi doctors did, I opened my private office in the evenings from four till eight p.m. to supplement my salary, which at that time was twenty-four Iraqi dinars, or ninety dollars a month.

I have to say a word about my housekeeping arrangement living in very primitive places as far as comforts, such as food and laundry and other needs are concerned when I was so busy with work. In 1954 my parents employed a young man named Peter to work with our cook Martha in Baghdad. Martha was getting older and no longer able to do the work alone. Peter was about nineteen years old. He learned how to cook, clean, and iron. He was a smart young man who could read and write but had dropped out of school to get a job. My mother was thinking that Peter might agree to accompany me in my new life to see the world when I started serving in rural areas. I don't think many mothers were so concerned to that degree.

After finishing my training, Peter was ready and excited. Luckily, I had an extra room for him. My mother insisted that I take with me a steamer trunk that my father bought during his trip to Europe in 1926. The trunk had languished in our storage room all that time awaiting such an opportunity to be useful. The trunk was like a walking wardrobe, it stood on its base and opens sideways. On one side I hung my pants and a couple of jackets and on the other side there were five small drawers for underwear. It was not big enough but proved to be very useful in those early days.

Peter did the grocery shopping and developed a good relationship with the locals, which made both our lives easier. In addition, he cooked, did my laundry and cleaned the house to my mother's standard. In the afternoon, he helped in my clinic by keeping an eye on the patients, helping them to come to the office when their turn comes up. He also helped almost like a secretary in other jobs around the house. For me, he was God sent.

Saddat al Hindiyah was only one hour from my parents in Baghdad. Having a house that was recently built with all the amenities made travelling to Baghdad not necessary more frequently than once every fortnight.

When I started working as a doctor, I thought that having had such a well-rounded education and training I could tackle any medical problem with ease. As the days rolled by, I learnt to be humble, and often needed to call other colleagues to ask for advice. Within about two months, I began to gain more confidence and more patients.

The patients who had not had a doctor before were coming by carloads and, at times, on donkeys, but mostly on foot. As the days went by, my services to the community became more and more appreciated and my office was always crowded. I was seeing forty to fifty patients each day. Those who could not pay for the visits came to the free public outpatient clinic, whereas those who could pay chose to seek my private clinic. The majority were poor.

Due to distance to Baghdad and my biweekly trips to my family and friends I needed to buy a small car. Having driven a Volkswagen Beetle once, I thought that it will be a very practical choice. That was my first car ever, purchased in 1956. The car cost eight hundred Iraqi dinars, which was equal to two thousand dollars at the time. Although I liked my work, I looked forward to my trips to Baghdad where I would meet with my friends and spend time with my family.

An incident occurred on one of my trips home that I still shudder to recall. My brother, Farouq, asked me if I had an antibiotic because he had a prolonged cold with an unremitting cough. I had penicillin in my black medical bag. I asked him if he had taken penicillin before and he said, "Yes, several times." I asked if he'd had an allergic reaction to it and he assured me he hadn't. I gave him an intramuscular injection and was about ready to leave his bedroom when he shouted, "Widad, I don't feel good." I looked at him and his skin was blanched. A sense of panic overwhelmed me. I had no antidote.

Immediately I thought of our family doctor who lived two streets away, that he'd likely have an adrenaline injection in his bag, it was nine at night, but I called his house.

"Doctor, do you have an ampule of adrenaline?" He said yes. "Please grab one and draw it into a syringe, and stand outside your house, I'm coming immediately. I'll explain later."

I jumped in my car and floored it, knowing it was a life or death situation. The doctor was there; I grabbed the syringe and flew back. When I ran into the bedroom my brother was status extremus, almost comatose, sweaty and pale. I stabbed the intramuscular shot into his shoulder, and we waited. His pulse was thready, and his eyes were closed. My father was wringing his hands over my nearly unresponsive brother. I was crying.

About one minute later Farouq opened his eyes, his pulse stronger, and he asked, "What happened?" I nearly collapsed with relief, as did our father. Of course, after that day Farouq knew that he had a penicillin allergy.

Back at Saddat al Hindiyah, a neighboring town had an Egyptian doctor who took care of a larger community, but he was not happy there and wanted to transfer to a bigger city. Having been educated in Egypt, he was not indebted to the government to place him and he could leave when he wished. And so he did, the day after informing the Ministry of Health of his decision. There was no replacement at such short notice. I was asked to cover his duties on a temporary basis, which added a lot of responsibilities and hours to my work.

My new duties included a small hospital of twelve beds. With the hospital came a female nurse and two male assistant nurses. The hospital served the immediate needs of the community. We treated severe infections, heart conditions, normal deliveries and minor surgical problems. The nurse was a trained midwife and so many women would ask her to go to their homes to deliver their babies. We even did tooth extractions.

As a team, it was amazing to see how much we could achieve. I even wrote a paper about intravenous use of iron in severely anemic patients. The paper was published in the Iraqi Medical Journal. I used intravenous iron in a drip form and gave multiple dosages at the same time. The first patient I treated for severe anemia had a hemoglobin level of 7gL which was critical. He needed a blood transfusion which we did not have. The twelve-year-old boy's family could not take him to Baghdad for that purpose and we did not have the equipment. He was severely infested with Ankylostomas. He showed fast improvement with no serious side effects which encouraged me to use the treatment frequently in similar cases.

My weekends became fewer and further-in-between because of the new responsibilities. I could not go to Baghdad as often and therefore could not see my friends and family except rarely. What was more tormenting was my inability to see my girlfriend with whom I had a secret relationship not known to my family or friends. I have to write about this relationship as it describes the life of young people at that time in the Middle East.

The story of my girlfriend started when I was still in my residency and when life was no more than work and learning. One night I was called to the emergency room to help. A small bus brought about twenty female boarding school seniors for treatment of acute food poisoning. They were in varying degrees of distress. Some came for treatment for the poisoning and some came for the fun of the trip. The doctor on duty asked me to do the triage thus giving me exposure to all those ladies.

One of them was more interested in talking with me than describing her symptoms. She was a beautiful outspoken girl who pretended to be interested in what was taking place in the emergency room and had a lot of questions for me to answer. After all the necessary measures were completed, the bus took the girls back to school leaving only two who needed to be admitted to the hospital.

I thought that the whole evening must have been a dream since all of the girls were Muslims and they were not wearing the usual black long cover and none of them had any compunction about talking with strangers without their mothers present. Of course, they had two female teachers as chaperones. The other doctor and I woke up from the dream and tried to go back to our work.

Twenty-four hours later I was called to answer a phone call. The caller was none other than the girl who left my mind in a whirlwind the night before. She introduced herself, as if that was necessary, and told me she would like to see me again. I almost fainted to hear this scary—and on her part—reckless suggestion. I told her that it was a crazy and suicidal idea but also a tantalizing offer.

I asked her if she was serious and if she had thought of the consequences to her, her family, and to me. She said she has been thinking of nothing else. In fact, I too had not thought of anything else. I was totally smitten by that daring and beautiful girl who engaged me in a long and irrelevant conversation. Her two teachers who escorted the students on the bus were observing us immersed in an exchange without any previous acquaintance. For me that was very unusual.

That was Baghdad in 1956 where society did not permit any relationship between man and woman without chaperones. To be seen together without a chaperon could jeopardize the girl's, and her family's reputation. It was even more dangerous to associate with a Muslim girl if you are not a Muslim. This was mostly a tribal tradition which became colored with a religious garb over the years. In the Middle East, especially in rural areas, tribal rules had long been the cornerstone of all human interaction. Honor in a member of a tribe is what the family lives by and what it's valued for. Honor in the tribal system is based on courage in war and raiding, generosity, and the virtue of the family's women.

Muslim women were not allowed to speak or interact with strangers without a chaperone, usually a mother or another member of the family. A girl who breached the tribal/religious rules not only fails in her religious responsibilities but taints the honor of the family in the eyes of society. She brings shame on her tribe to the point where her parents lose their standing in the tribe. Even her siblings would be shunned and become unworthy of the respect of other families.

If a girl became pregnant before marriage, she was treated as a source of disgrace and dishonor. It was a death sentence where a male member of the family had to restore honor to the tribe or family, by killing the girl. Sometimes even the male partner who brought on this dishonor on the tribe may pay with his life for this kind of insult. Dating in the Muslim world was, and probably still is, unheard of and is against all religious and tribal rules.

I was certain that my caller knew from my language that I was a Christian. Furthermore, I was sure that she was familiar with the rules of society and the consequences of being caught red-handed. When I asked her as to how, when, and where she proposed to meet, she said that is the second hurdle we will both have to plan. She told me that there are limitations to this relationship if it happens. The most important condition was to accept that the relationship is to be platonic. I realized then that this girl had done a lot of thinking about the parameters of our future relationship. I agreed that that was understood by both for obvious reasons. We were already swept away with the excitement of the possibility. We started planning how to bring this idea to reality. We talked about where and how to meet.

The proposition became a challenge. We forgot about the consequences and began to talk about how to bring this project to life. We had to find safe places to meet and how to call each other without raising suspicions. After the second call we were both ready to start this wonderful story of platonic love and romance. We wrote long letters and beautiful poetry, we stole kisses, we held hands, and we embraced. We were in love. She was nineteen and I was twenty-five. She had just graduated from high school. And I had just graduated from medical school and the army. It was my first experience with love. Much has been written in the Arabic language about unfulfilled love. She was the reason I looked forward to going to Baghdad, in addition to visiting with my family. My new little car was of great help in getting around when my girlfriend was allowed to go out for various excuses.

Looking back on my adventures with this girl I wonder about our most precarious experience. It could have spelt doom for both of us. One quiet evening she and I were sitting on a bench in a distant part of a park in Baghdad, feeling safe and distant from the public eye. We were engrossed in a quiet conversation when suddenly we were jolted as the bushes about ten feet from us parted with the vicious shouts of two armed policeman. "What are you doing in the park after hours?" It was 7:10 p.m. and the park had closed at 7 p.m. We were shaken up and terrified, not only because of the drama of the police materializing in that fashion, but of the possibility of being discovered by our families and by our community. Our fear turned into terror when these men insisted on taking us to the police station.

I gathered all my courage and told them we did not mean to break the law, but that did not make a dent in the situation. I told them I was a captain in the medical corps of the army. They did not budge. By then my friend was almost wailing, pleading with me to solve the problem. I remembered I had money in my pocket.

I apologized to the policemen and added that I would like to reward them for their vigilance and offered them 10 Dinars, (about 34 dollars), to make up for their time and assured them that we would never stay past the legal time again, if they would just allow us to go home. (At that time, that amount was equal to about one month's pay for one of them.) Surprisingly, they promptly accepted and escorted us to the gate of the park. Later on, I realized that the whole thing was a routine performance by those two policemen to supplement their salaries. For the two of us it was an awful experience which helped to make us more aware of the risks of our relationship.

It was a horrifying evening for both of us. However, it did not deter her from making plans a few weeks later to visit me at my village. She was very creative in finding a plan and shocked me by wanting to travel four hours by train to visit me where I worked. That was very frightening to me. Not only was she going to take the train alone in the middle of the night, but she was going to stay overnight away from home without a chaperone. If her adventure and her excuse were discovered, both of our lives would have been in real danger, especially hers. I tried to dissuade her, but to no avail. She told me that I worried too much.

I informed Peter that I expected a confidential visitor and that no one could be told of this visit in the small town or in Baghdad. The train arrived at five a.m. in a station fifteen minutes from my small village. We had a train station in Saddat al Hindiyah, but she thought it would be better for me to meet her in her chosen station. It goes without saying that being a perpetual worrier, I stood in the train station almost frozen with fear not believing that she would be on that train. The train stopped on time and the doors opened and there she was carrying a small valise beaming with joy. She said she was the only passenger in that compartment. We drove back to my house just as the sun was rising. It was a weekend as weekends go in Iraq: Thursday afternoon to Saturday morning. That Friday proved to be one of the greatest days in my life.

She told me that her mother has a sister in a town on the same train route but about one hour further along than my town. She told her mother that she wanted to go visit the aunt who has no phone and the family meets every few years. Women usually make these arrangements. *Unfortunately,* her mother was unable to go with her. She said her mother took her to the station and will pick her up on Saturday morning, "Inshallah," which in Arabic means "God willing."

The year we spent together with the pain, the love, and the fears were glorious days that ended suddenly. She came to me crying one day and told me that her father had informed her that a very nice man, a distant relative, had asked for her hand in marriage. She had no choice in the matter as tradition went in the tribal system.

My world crashed. I felt depressed and confused; I lost my joy and excitement in life. I knew we had no choice. There was no way to compete by offering what the cousin could offer. Being Christian I could not hope to be accepted over the other suitor. We were centuries apart in a world we did not create, and we had no power to change. We stopped seeing and calling each other. I knew that she was going through the same pain.

She started to go to a pharmacy that belonged to my cousin and sit and sob. My cousin, who knew about our secret because we used her pharmacy sometimes to meet, would tell me. What happened was expected, we were un-able to stop it. All we had left were the beautiful but painful memories, the yearning, and the sense of hopelessness. It took a long time to compose myself and move on with my life. As I muse over the past, it haunts me still.

I balanced my sadness with the responsibilities of my work. I was lucky to be so busy that I didn't have enough time to think. Life had to go on and my patients expected my full attention. I delved into work and between the two communities, I had no time to think about girl-friends or about love.

I remember around that time I was asked by my mother whether I was interested in marriage now that I finished college and was financially independent, a ques-tion that came up often. I always answered that I was not ready. I was 26 going on 27. My work became my obsession. I had to organize two clinics and a hospital by establishing specific hours for children and hours for adults. With my team we developed hours for tuberculosis patients, pa-tients with infectious and parasitic conditions and patients with other chronic conditions in addition to all other acute problems. My male assistant nurse had some experience in pulling out teeth. I did a lot of sutures, and minor wound care.

What made my stay in that town special after the increase of work and my loss of interest in frequently going to Baghdad was the fact that I could invite my whole family to visit for picnics, that later were remembered by everyone who could come. Apart from my parents and siblings, I had cousins, an uncle and his wife and their children and others.

As it happened, the dam had to be blocked from time to time, which meant the fish from upstream were trapped making it possible for the fishermen to have a hay day with their catch when it happened. They would catch the fish and tie a lot of the big ones measuring over two feet in length with their hooks and lines to the side of their boats still alive in the water. When buyers come to shop, they will have live fish recently caught.

When I planned to have my family over, they came in four or five cars and we gathered in a large outdoor casino/park that I rented for the day. The seating area overlooked the dam and the river, giving us a unique view of the site. The fish that I had ordered was called *shabboot*. They were from the same family as carp and were very tasty and prized in Iraq. They were cooked in the open air after cleaning them from all their entrails and standing them on their sides with skewers in a semi-circle. A fire was started in a place very close to the fish allowing the breeze to be directed at the fish. When the fish were cooked, they were taken off the skewers and placed in large trays with their insides facing up. A special sauce made of tomato juice, garlic, salt, pepper, and curry amongst other spices, was spread all over it to give it a great taste.

With the fish usually came fresh baked tandoori, kebob, bread, salads and other foods and a variety of drinks. Usually everybody had a good time enjoying the scenery, the food, and the fellowship. They headed home late in the evening and talked about the visit for years. My parents, my siblings and cousins always had a good time.

All my days in Saddat al Hindiyah were not enjoyable, however. There were some very trying times that caused me a great deal of worry and fear. Such as the evening when I was seeing patients in my private office and a car stopped outside and four men wearing Bedouin garb pulled another man in his twenties out of the car. He was barely able to stand up by himself. He was brought directly to my examining room when the other patients realized that there was an emergency.

The oldest man in the group informed me that his son had been running a fever for the last two days. They were alarmed, however, when he stopped eating and worse, when he was unable to drink. He would choke when he tried to drink. They said there were no others in the family who had these symptoms. In taking a history they did not have anything helpful. The patient was not very alert. He had a temperature of one hundred and three, and was dehydrated. He asked for water, but in a garbled way. I asked the father if his son was bitten by an animal in the previous two months and he answered promptly in the negative. My nurse brought him a glass of water to drink, he looked at it eagerly, but when the glass was close to his mouth he began to choke. His throat was going through spasms so severe that he could not drink.

Hydrophobia is the name of that reaction. Translated from Greek, it means fear of water, a well-known symptom of rabies. I told the father that his son had rabies, and I explained to him that the condition had no treatment and that it was invariably fatal. At that time the number of documented victims who survived could be counted on one hand. The father persisted in his denial of a bite. Later I heard from outside sources that it was rumored in the area that he was bitten by a wolf.

The family was advised that I didn't have any treatment for their son, but I could give them some sedatives to calm him down in case he became violent, or they could take him to Baghdad for a second opinion. They did not want to take him home or to Baghdad, they requested me to admit him to the small hospital in the neighboring town to give fluids and sedatives. The hospital was about ten minutes away from my village. The town had probably about three thousand inhabitants, and the hospital had twelve beds.

I arranged for the young man to be admitted and ordered intravenous fluids and a sedative. At two o'clock in the morning someone was ringing my outside bell and banging on the door. I went to the door and found two men, one wore a police uniform and the other was a civilian. Both were screaming at me to hurry up and go with them to the hospital. They told me that the patient I admitted that evening was uncontrollable, attacking the staff and the patients.

When we arrived at the hospital, we found the inpatients had left their beds, and were standing out in the hospital yard, some with their IV stands. All were in a state of terror. There were two policemen, who at that time were the entire cadre of the town's police force, standing between the patients and the gentleman in question. That man was standing at the entrance of the hospital building, twirling the steel stand that holds the hand washbasin. The stand weighed not less than twenty pounds. He was delirious and scared and thought that we were going to hurt him.

I felt that talking him down would be a waste of time. I sent the two policemen to the back door of the hospital and directed them to come from behind him while I and the male nurse kept him occupied until the two policemen grabbed him from the back. After that, we restrained him, and took him back to his bed and gave him a sedative. Most of the patients refused to go back to their beds for the rest of the night. After the sedation started to work, I put him back on I.V. fluids and drove back home.

It was almost six o'clock in the morning when my nurse called from the hospital. He informed me that the patient passed away half an hour earlier. He added with some alarm that there were about twenty armed men wanting to take the body for burial. I told him we cannot release the body without an autopsy according to the Iraqi health regulations.

He said, "With due respect doctor, I will leave this to you to tell them."

I could understand why he didn't want to be involved, being a tribesman himself. So, I had to rush back to explain the legal situation to the family.

The scene when I arrived was like a military siege. I had to push myself with a lot of trepidation through these angry men who were holding their guns with muzzles pointing up. I asked to talk to the father of the deceased in my office. The man came in with his other son, who had helped bring his brother to my office the evening before. The father told me as soon as he got inside my office that the tribe follows tribal law rather than the government law. He said that in Islam a dead person has to be buried the same day of the death. Furthermore, his religion forbid autopsy for "whatever reason." He added, "The men outside are all cousins and other relatives who will kill if necessary, to do what their religion dictates."

The man was very convincing when one considered the gun power outside. I became very interested in letting him take his son and leave rather than take my life. But I had no authority to disobey the law. I called the regional medical officer and described to him the drama outside the hospital gates. There was a slight delay and then he told me that the tribe's presentation was very convincing and that he would prefer to have a living doctor in that hospital than a dead man who was in need of an autopsy.

Based on his wise judgment, I let the family follow the edict of their religion and have their son to bury. That was my first, but not the last, encounter with tribal customs. It was very difficult for me to determine then which law really dictates the rules, the government or the tribes. Even now it is very difficult to separate the blurred boundaries between the two.

Another interesting accident occurred while I was practicing in Saddat al Hindiyah. One day while I was driving back from Baghdad to my office in that town, I had to slow down through the small village of Mahmodiyah. The highway ran through a rather crowded area where a median walkway of about six feet in width and six inches in height had recently been built. I saw a man about fifteen feet away standing on the walkway waiting to cross the street.

In my mind, I noted his presence and made a point of slowing down. However, as I was beside him, he suddenly stepped forward and crashed into the side of my car, as if he was completely unaware of the traffic. He hit my outside mirror which threw him back onto the walkway with a thud. I stopped the car as fast as I could and created an instant traffic jam so I could run back to the man who was still on the ground.

As I looked at him moaning and waving his hands in the air, I realized he was totally blind. I was shocked by the accident and by his misfortune. I told him I was very sorry about what happened, and realized a huge crowd had gathered around us, giving me another serious problem to contend with. A policeman appeared from nowhere trying to figure out what happened while he calmed the crowd.

As I told the policeman about the accident, I saw the blind man trying to get up pointing to his hip. He screamed in pain. The crowd grew angrier, screaming at each other and me, shouting for justice and revenge. I thought I'd be assaulted. Apparently, this blind beggar was someone well known to them, as they passed him every day. After telling the policeman who I was and what had happened, I asked the policeman to help me put the injured man in my car as I knew there was no ambulance in that town. I then drove through the angry crowd to the small local hospital and talked to the doctor that I suspected a broken hip. It was getting late by the time I finished reporting to the police chief at the station, so I called my office from there. This, of course was 1956. Doctors had no smartphones, not even pocket phones. In fact, there were probably only two or three phones in that whole town, perhaps only in government offices.

When I went to see the patient the next day, they had already diagnosed his broken hip and called a local surgeon to help. He told me that his only income was from panhandling. He supported his wife and two very young grandchildren. I told him I would support his family until he was able to go back to work. It was three months before he could go back to his known spot. He was in the hospital for two months.

Four months later as I was driving to my work from Baghdad, the same policeman stopped me and told me the old man I'd injured wanted to talk to me. I walked to where he was, he struggled to stand up and he kissed my hand, thanking me for all I did for his family. Every two or three weeks after that accident when I passed through that town I stopped and gave him a few dinars for his family.

A different, though equally memorable situation occurred not too long after, and brought me face to face with a similar conundrum. It happened one evening when I was about to go to bed. A car stopped in front of my house and the doorbell rang soon after. Two youngish men dressed in expensive Arabic garb saluted respectfully and told me, "The sheikh's daughter has fallen ill and is in pain and the sheikh requests you to help her."

They added that they have the sheikh's car to take me there and bring me back. That was a request one can never refuse. A sheikh is the ruler, the great father, the wise one, the leader of the area tribe. The ones that I came to know and sometimes to respect and like were very wise. Many of them were very knowledgeable in matters of politics and life in general.

I got ready and left with them. The trip was not long, and the sheikh's entourage was waiting for me. They opened the car door for me and led me to the reception room where the sheikh was waiting. We were left alone, and they closed the door behind them. I knew the gentleman from before when I treated him for a minor problem. He offered me a cigarette which was the usual part of the hospitality routine and then tea was brought by one of the men who were outside.

In the meantime, my host asked after my health and thanked me for responding to his request. When we were left alone again, he explained to me that his wife, the mother of the sick girl, was worried about her daughter who had been complaining of stomach pains and had not been eating. In fact, he added that she had been vomiting intermittently. She was fourteen. A sense of doom overwhelmed me as I began to run in my mind the possible diagnoses that I could think of taking into consideration the mother's worry and the girl's age.

The most worrisome problem that mothers worry about in that culture was pregnancy of an unmarried daughter which will reflect on her and on the husband and the tribe. And as a physician, I wanted to keep my objectivity and reach an accurate diagnosis, and of course be of help to the patient.

I was ushered to the harem where the patient and her mother and two other women were waiting. All the women were covered except for their eyes. The patient was in bed. The mother and the other women appeared to have been crying. The mother repeated the father's story.

I was allowed to examine the girl with her long dress on. By then I had learned the protocol of examining female Muslim patients in Iraq. Inspection had to be dispensed with. Palpation can only be done with the patient fully dressed. On occasions (always with a female chaperone) the chaperone will expose a minimum area of the chest for the stethoscope to touch the skin. As happened that night, the mother trying to be helpful, allowed me to adequately examine her daughter.

The girl was old enough to understand the tragic situation that she and her parents were going to go through should there be a suspicion of pregnancy in the diagnosis. Under the circumstances, it was impossible to ask the natural question as to whether there was a history of sexual relations. The girl was assumed to be a virgin. The mother intimated to me that the girl had not had a period for two or three months. The mother was very scared and kept asking if I knew what was wrong with her daughter. I knew that the mother had a good idea.

At the end of my examination I wrote a prescription for something to reduce the vomiting and told the mother that her daughter needed to go to Baghdad in the morning to see a specialist as I couldn't be sure what the problem was. I gave her the name and address of an obstetrician who I knew and felt sure she would try and salvage the situation. The mother would, if she knew the truth, have to discuss with the female obstetrician what can be done to save the daughter's life and the family's and tribal honor. As I mentioned earlier, honor, generosity and courage during war or raids are the three main measures that the tribal worth is based on. Honor is mostly placed on the women of the tribe and their behavior within the tribal and family rules.

Two years before that night and while I was still a resident, I had a firsthand experience with what can happen to a naïve teenage girl if she is abused by a member of her family, usually a brother or a cousin since her world in that kind of environment is restricted to those males. I had been called to see a young woman who was admitted to the medical unit in a state of terror. Her heart was racing, she was sweating, looked terrified, and she could not stop crying. After we sedated her, I was able to talk to her and she told me her story.

She was born in one of the southern districts of Iraq. She was allowed to go to school until the fourth grade, just enough to learn to read and write and do simple math. Her family promised her to her cousin when she reached the age of fourteen. Regrettably, her cousin could not wait, living in the same home; he prevailed on her or forced her to have sex with him as she was going to be his wife in a year anyway. She got pregnant and when she told him about it, he told her that it was her fault. She realized that she was going to be killed by her family for having disgraced them and their tribe including the perpetrator. Her only choice was to run away to Baghdad. Having no money and no place to live she found her way to a brothel where she managed to survive for two or three years.

Of course, that is a common story amongst girls who, out of desperation, fall into the wrong hands and can't find their way out. Shortly before she came to the hospital, she heard that her brother had been looking for her since she ran away and now knew where she was. Someone from her tribe recognized her and told the family. The horror of what she knew was going to happen to her led her to the hospital with the hope of hiding or getting help of some kind.

I called the senior resident and told him the story. We changed her name in the records and whisked her to a private room totally out of the way and we even asked two nurses to keep their eyes on the room. The next morning the girl was found dead. Her brother had followed her to the hospital and found an opportunity to sneak into her room and stabbed her savagely several times. The honor of the family had been restored.

Many years later when I came back to Iraq from England after studying psychiatry, I was destined to see what happens to those men who are compelled to 'wash' the honor of the family with the blood of their daughters, their sisters or their wives. The duty of every adult or even a teen boy is to restore the honor of the tribe. This was not a religious duty, it was a tribal duty. It was the way men controlled women. (I believe this tradition still exists in our world, even in the USA where immigrant families bring their brutal tribal culture to the new world.)

One afternoon in 1965, a man came to my private psychiatric office in Baghdad. He looked preoccupied and very agitated. He was about forty years old. He was dressed in western style. He looked intelligent and well spoken. As soon as he sat down and told me his name and age he burst into tears and soon he was sobbing. He finally calmed himself and told me that his wife wanted him to come and see me because he was falling apart. He could not sleep, he could not eat, and he could not stop crying.

His story began about seven months before when his wife told him that she suspected their fourteen-year-old daughter and the apple of his eye, was pregnant. The mother was sure because the daughter confided in her and asked her to help her. The daughter refused to identify the perpetrator. Panic set in the family. There were two younger brothers who should never know anything about this tragedy. All the girl was willing to say in a state of terror was that it was not her fault. She cried and shook and realized what the situation meant.

The father sitting in front of me cried quietly and told me that he worked in a government job. He belonged to the tribe that covered the area where he worked. He was highly respected for having achieved his position in the government. The tribe was proud of him. He knew what had to be done to salvage his honor and his boys' future. Some people he knew faced a similar dilemma and chose to quietly arrange for an abortion. But he said the news had spread out and that family was living in shame. He had to do the "right" thing for his family's honor.

He told his daughter and his wife one morning that he was taking her to Baghdad to stay with an aunt. The aunt would keep the secret and take care of the girl until birth and then she would give the baby up for adoption. On the way to her aunt's home, the daughter, who was very scared, asked him, "Where are you taking me, Dad?" He said he almost went back home when she asked, "Did you lie to me? Are you going to kill me?" He had to do the honorable thing. He buried his precious daughter in the desert sand and went back home. His wife knew what he had to do and knew that for the rest of his life he will have his honor amongst men, but he would never forget what he did for that honor.

When he finished his story, he and I were both shaking. He was sobbing, and I was barely holding back my tears. There was no consolation for this grief and there was no solace. I had no medicine that I could give to that man to relieve his agony. I let him talk and cry until he settled down. All I could give him was something to help him sleep and an anti-depressant. That man needed to be in a hospital, but that would have been another dishonor to be known as a mentally ill person.

It was during that story that I remembered that poor innocent girl that I had to send to Baghdad to face her cruel world about six years earlier and the girl who, in the security of the hospital that she trusted, had lost her life to save somebody's dubious honor.

That session surprisingly also brought back to me a forgotten memory when I was six years old. I remembered that one night at bedtime I heard a woman wailing and screaming in a piercing way as if she was in terrible agony. The voice was not far from our house. I woke up my father who told me he did not know what it was: perhaps a family fight. In the morning we heard that a young woman was killed in our neighborhood. My parents exchanged knowing looks. Apparently, that woman was killed by her brother. Memories of that tribal savagery still haunt me all these years later.

Another very traumatic experience that troubled me for many years and kept me awake for many nights was the case of the five-year-old girl who was brought by her parents to my private office in Sadat al Hindiyah one night at about ten o'clock.

The girl was unconscious and had been seizing for the previous three hours. The parents told me that she woke up in the morning with fever and they were giving her baby aspirin. Apparently, the fever continued to rise until the evening when she began to seize. They tried to reduce her temperature by applying cold towels to her head and limbs, but nothing happened.

On exam, the poor little girl was unconscious but very fidgety and twitchy. We were unable to arouse the girl. Her fever was about one hundred and five degrees, her pulse was one hundred and eighty-eight per minute, and she was dehydrated. I knew that I was facing a potentially lethal situation. The only thing that I had was Phenobarbital I.M. That was before the time of the modern meds that we use now intravenously. We tried to cool the girl by wrapping her with wet blankets. I gave her an injection of Phenobarbital and Dilantin and waited. Dilantin is very slow in reaching the brain. Nothing seemed to change; her seizures continued one after the other with only a few minutes in between. Finally, I asked the father, who was a government employee, to drive the girl to Baghdad Royal Hospital.

For a physician, knowing that the condition he is dealing with is controllable, but he does not have what he needs to treat it, is the most destructive and agonizing situation that he can face. For days, I had difficulty focusing on my work. I did not know what happened to the little girl. I heard nothing from the parents and my mind was wavering between the thought that she may have recovered or that she did not survive. I finally had to calm myself to where I was able to go back to work. Until now, I still wonder about the fate of that little girl.

One more memorable incident that I vividly remember is the story of the *guffa*. One afternoon after a hectic day at the clinic, the temperature a sizzling one hundred and ten, my doorbell rang. When I opened the door, there before me stood a man who appeared to be very nervous and disheveled.

I asked him how I could help him. He hurriedly told me he wanted me to come with him to examine his wife because she was critically ill. I asked if he could bring her to the clinic, but he said she was much too sick to move. When I asked him where he lived, he answered that it wasn't far, and that he'd hired a cab to take us there. I realized it must be a serious case, not too close—otherwise why the cab? I dreaded to leave at two in the heat of the afternoon, but I felt I had to go. I was often asked to see older patients or very sick ones at their homes.

I grabbed my medical bag that contained everything I would need for any emergency. We got in the cab and the driver pulled out in a hurry. After about ten minutes, I asked the man how much farther until we reached his house. And he reassured me that it was not too far. Ten minutes later I repeated my question and got the same answer. Finally, after another ten minutes, the cab stopped at the side of a roaring river. The man got out and wanted to carry my bag, but I declined his offer, lest we damage something. Looking around me I saw no signs of homes or people in the area. He informed me that we had to cross the river. But there were no boats, as I knew them, in sight and there was no bridge. There was, however, a rope tied tightly to the two poles on either side of the river.

The desert sun was hitting us directly, there was no shade, and my back was hurting from carrying my heavy bag. I was miserable. The scared husband revealed that the only way to his house was across the river in a *guffa* which could barely hold three people. I worried; I knew I couldn't swim well enough to tackle a fast river. (A *guffa* is a round tub-like boat, made of reeds from the river banks, tightly woven in several layers and then covered with tar, until it was waterproof. That one was only large enough for two passengers and the boat owner, who pulled us across the river, hand-over-hand using the rope.)

The young father carried my bag the last mile to his home. It was a small hut with a low opening for a door. Of course, there was no electricity or running water. In the little available light, I saw four bodies on the floor of the hut. One was his wife, and the others were their three children between the ages of two and five. My exam for all four took only twenty minutes. They all had pneumonia. I gave them all injections of penicillin. I gave the father prescriptions to buy medications for his family.

By then we were on the verge of collapse from the heat. But we had to walk back to the *guffa*, cross the river, and drive back home. It took only twenty-five minutes to solve the problem, but four hours of travel in the heat. The young man thanked me profusely and apologized for not having money to pay me. He offered me all that was in his pockets; he had a quarter of a dinar, the equivalent of twenty-five cents. I asked him to use it to buy his prescriptions. Two days later he returned to the clinic to report that his family was better already. He was profusely thankful. I learned not to believe patients who claimed they lived close, and I learned how to cross the river in a *guffa*.

My year of service in that village came to its end. I was waiting for the government to let me know where I was going to go next, when I received a letter from the Ministry of Health saying that the people of that village sent some tribal dignitaries to Baghdad asking the minister of health to keep me in their village for another year.

There was a condition to that order, though. They also wanted me to officially take over the responsibility of covering the small hospital and clinic in the neighboring town. As I mentioned earlier, the responsible doctor had resigned, and they thought I could become the official physician for both areas. The job was already streamlined and going smoothly, having worked out the details with my team when I started covering for the other doctor, so I accepted the position for another year.

# The Man from Baghdad

My trips to Baghdad every two or three weeks were also very memorable events not only because I was eager to see my family and friends, but because they exposed me to the real Iraq that I never quite knew before. Although I knew a lot of the history of my country, I had lived a rather sheltered life in Baghdad as I grew up.

Driving through the countryside and being close to the everyday people opened my eyes to the poverty, the system of government and the everyday toil of the overwhelming majority of the citizens of this ancient civilization. Central Iraq on both sides of the two great rivers (the Tigris and the Euphrates) is a very fertile land that was tilled and has provided enough food for millions of people over centuries of rule by various empires. It was those people—living then and now as their ancestors had—who sweated and toiled to give our city dwellers the food they consume every day of their lives. If these men were not employed in government jobs in their areas, their main chance of survival was farming the land. Most of them went to school at least until they were able to read and write, but to have a real job you needed a high school certificate. As one passes from one bucolic scene to another, one appreciates the hard labor and the poverty of these people.

Iraq at that time was beginning to rise and wake up to what was needed to bring about a better life for the citizens. But one coup after the other hampered these efforts.

It was during this second year of medical service in Saddat al Hindiyah that I experienced my second serious epidemic. This time it was smallpox.

To have an epidemic in an environment where people want to hide the scope of the situation is very thwarting to say the least. Fortunately, my staff and I were already vaccinated against smallpox. We hoped that we were safe. It gave us the confidence to enter peoples' homes to examine the known victims and to vaccinate the others.

We divided the town (the epidemic was in the second village that I was given to take care of) into small segments and began to spread information among the people by word of mouth. Some of the people who knew their kin to have the condition began to hide them in their homes. They knew what the illness could do to the skin, the eyes, and the brain and eventually to life.

I realized that for them to have this condition was a stigma and a dishonor. It was the same stigma that prevented the father of the young man who had rabies to tell me that his son was bitten by a wolf or coyote. Maybe it was a sense of shame, to have something that dangerous in their household. To allow a doctor or a nurse to examine their wives or daughters or even their sisters may have been more dishonorable than seeing the patients maimed or dead.

The epidemic was generalized, and it was spreading fast in the community. Children and adults were involved. Eventually the people saw what can happen to them and their loved ones. They opened their homes and begged us to help them. We hospitalized as many patients as we could.

Isolation of the sick and quarantining the contacts was the strategy to control the disease. Vaccination was our preventative measure. We knew that the vaccination effects take a long time, but it had to be done. Of course, we attended to all of the willing population, and hospitalized the infected ones. Our workers had to go to every home and vaccinate the young and old. Antibiotics were given to those who were clearly infected to minimize skin and eye infections.

But no real treatment was available at that time. The Mussayab epidemic was in the winter of 1958. It took a couple of months before the epidemic was controlled. The winter season was not helpful since people needed to stay inside their cottages to remain warm. We had to ask for help from Baghdad due to the number of people to be vaccinated quickly. We lost three or four patients; one of them was an infant.

At the end of two years in the area of Mussayab and Saddat al Hindiyah, I was ready for another move to where the government felt I was needed.

Dr. Widad Bazzoui in Sadat al Hindiyah.

## Chapter Five

# Medicine in the Desert

I received a letter from the Ministry of Health about a month before the end of my second year. I was asked to prepare to go to another rural area called Mansuryah, a town unfamiliar to me.

After asking around, as it was not on the map, I was told that the only reason people knew it was because a very powerful sheikh lived there. It was described as a very small village that does not have even a store. To get to it, one had to drive two hours on a dusty road in the desert in central Iraq. I was told that it had no running water and no electricity, and all the houses were built from mud. The description was very worrisome for my family. For me it was a new adventure. The town was built on both sides of the Khalis River, a tributary to the mighty Tigris River.

My mother's cousin, who also came from Aleppo, owned a Mercedes agency in Baghdad. He used to visit us frequently and listen to my stories about my work. He told my mother that there was a new Mercedes model specially made for desert driving. It had a higher chassis, it was dust-proof, and had air conditioning. He said that he could sell it to me at cost. That's when I sold my first small car and bought a Mercedes 219. It was a luxury car to be sure.

On the last weekend of my two-year service, I took my new black car and Peter, and we headed for this distant land that was going to be my home for at least one year. We took with us enough baggage for a few days. It was a sunny spring day. Spring in Iraq lasts about a month followed by rapidly warming summer that often lasts until the end of November.

I had a lot of confidence in my Mercedes, though. It drove beautifully on paved roads, but the roads we were going to cover were dirt roads and very bumpy. The dust that it stirred up was sucked in by the air conditioner and delivered to the inside of the sedan, despite what the relative had told us. Pretty soon we were inhaling it with every breath, so I turned off the air and opened the windows which I felt was an improvement. After about an hour of driving I noticed that daylight was gradually dimming.

Neither Peter nor I understood what was happening until we began to be hit by locusts from all sides, and before long the desert in front of us was covered by millions, if not billions, of those well-nourished critters. Of course, we rolled the windows up, but that did not stop them from getting in. They were coming in through the air conditioning vents.

By then we were driving on a thick layer of crunchy insects covering acres of desert, moving, flying, hitting the windshield and bumper, while thousands were being crushed by the car. To stop meant that we would be buried by this plague, so we continued to drive to the best of our ability, until we finally drove out of this revolting cloud of locusts. I had heard about the locust invasions in North Africa and Egypt but to be inundated by this plague in central Iraq was demoralizing indeed, especially to have these billions of insects land on a desert where there was nothing for them to eat.

After a while we stopped the car and proceeded to rid the inside of the vehicle of these unwelcome, disgusting creatures. After another hour of driving we saw at a distance a big building with the Iraqi flag on a high pole which indicated the presence of the official director of the county. As we approached, we saw a policeman at the gate who was trying to organize his uniform and hat.

When we stopped, he stood at attention, and when I got out of the car, he gave me the usual military salute.

"At ease soldier," I said, and he relaxed.

To him anybody crazy enough to drive a brand-new fancy black car to a Godforsaken place like that must surely be a high government official; perhaps a high-ranking army officer or someone equal coming for an inspection. I asked him who the director was; he gave me his rank and name before he ran inside to announce my presence.

The name was familiar. I knew his brother from medical school. After introductions, he asked me what I was doing in that wilderness and I told him that I was there to provide medical care to the community. He said, "What community? All we have are about fifty or sixty mud shacks."

Then I showed him my letter of appointment and told him that it must be the sheikh who initiated the request for a doctor for his tribe. The director then called the sheikh. The sheikh was flustered at not having told the director about a request for a doctor, but he asked the director to take me to see him at his house.

We arrived at the sheikh's home and found him waiting for us. He was an elderly man who conveyed an air of dignity and confidence. I noticed he was dressed in formal Arab dress. Arab dress is the product of centuries of life with insufferable heat, drought, and frequent onslaughts of dust and windstorms. The main dress is called a *dishdasha* and is a long-sleeved shirt that goes down to the ground with a buttoned collar. Usually it is made of cotton and always in white. White is chosen against all logic in such a dusty environment due to its cooling effect, according to folklore.

On top of this dishdasha, the gentry and the well-to-do men wear a long coat open from the front very similar to a robe. It goes also to the ground. In winter, all men wear these coats, sometimes called a *jubba*. The rich men such as the sheikhs of Saudi Arabia use fine wool or cashmere. The less fortunate use cheaper wool, sometimes coarse wool spun by their women.

The headdress is very typical, almost idiosyncratic to the Arabs. They wear a large kerchief, pure white silk for the rich, patterned with black or red designs for the rest of the men. The kerchief covers the head, the ears, and reaches down to the shoulders. To hold it down, a black or golden-colored cord an inch in diameter is rolled in a circle or two on top of the head.

This sheikh of mine was wearing unpretentious attire, but still had the long shirt and the headdress.

He welcomed us and took us to his reception room where we sat on the pillows and rugs on the floor, an Arabic tradition. He proceeded to thank me in the usual elaborate tribal fashion, using compliments and incantations asking Allah to keep me healthy and successful. These salutations can become sometimes so elaborate to the point of tedium. After that, Peter and I were served tea. My servant then left us to talk privately.

The sheikh explained the reasons he asked for a doctor to serve in this distant area. He said that his tribe is composed of several related sub-tribes. Despite their blood relation, they are very contentious and feudal. The government relied on him to keep the men satisfied and ready to serve in case there is a revolt or a feud between the tribes. To do this he has to treat them equally. He had been marrying every couple of years a girl from a different smaller tribe. To stay on the right side of his religion he needed to divorce one of his four wives and send her to her family preferably pregnant. She would then give her tribe the distinction that they are kin to the sheikh. Something that reminded me of what the sheikhs of old Arabia did in the not-so-distant past.

He continued by saying that his tribe is increasing in size but not in wealth. They cannot travel to seek medical care due to distance and cost. He added that he was getting older and his ability to do his sexual duty to these

young women who are new in his life was getting less reliable. He needed a doctor to help him stay well and "fit."

At the end of our meeting, he told me that he had
asked his first, oldest and most highly respected wife to
move back to his house so I can use her relatively large
house for the clinic and for my personal residence. The
house was built of brick, had a large entry hall that would
serve as a waiting room. Two large rooms opened into this
entrance hall. One would be the pharmacy and the nursing
room. The other room would be partitioned into bedroom
and exam room. There was no room for my servant in this
arrangement.

We spent the night in the sheikh's house on mattresses on the floor. The next day we visited the future
clinic and headed back to Baghdad to bring what I would
need in medicines and a few pieces of furniture. I had to
take my servant/assistant/secretary home. My mother was
aware of this possibility and said he could have his old job
with the family. The furniture was meager due to the
smallness of what was to be my bedroom and living area.
Not having running water, electricity, or sewage was very
disconcerting to me.

My mother was suffering from breast cancer that
had metastasized to her lungs; at that time, she was literally fighting for her life. I did not want to let her know what
my new living arrangement was. She was beginning to
have difficulty breathing due to the emergence of bloody
effusion in the plural cavity pressing on the lungs and re-
stricting their expansion, and I didn't want to add to her
stress.

# The Man from Baghdad

Looking back, 1958 was a really bad year in many ways. My mother had come back at the beginning of the year from Beirut (Lebanon) having been treated with cobalt radiation and was showing no improvement. In fact, she was losing ground and in the previous three months she had lost a lot of weight and had begun to have difficulty breathing.

Unfortunately, it was easier for me to go home at the spur of the moment when I was in the previous village. The roads were paved, and I was able to be by her side in one hour. That would not be easy in my new placement. The first problem was that I had no one, not even a nurse's assistant to cover for me. In the second place, the trip was going to be two rough hours of unpaved roads to Baghdad.

I knew that she was not going to be with us for long. My father and siblings were in a very sad state looking at me for hope and support, and I was helpless in the face of a hopeless disease. I was determined to help her with her suffering as much as I could and be the support for the rest of my family.

My father, two sisters and brother tried to be with her all the time, but they were overwhelmed and in despair. I was the doctor in the family; she was the one who had insisted I would be a doctor. I tried to rise to everyone's expectations. My father was in terrible shape emotionally but was not able to show his true feelings to her or to my sisters who were absolutely terrified. They all had jobs and took turns caring for her and Peter our servant was a with her all the time.

# Widad E. Bazzoui

My mother was very sad and anxious to see me go to my new job. She knew that she did not have long to live. She depended on me to take care of her although she knew I may not be able to stay long with her. She was coming to the end and was in terrible shape. Her family physician could no longer help. She struggled for each breath. When I examined her before leaving for the new job, I found that she had fluid in her lungs causing the breathing difficulty. I called a colleague of mine and asked him to help me do a paracentesis, which would drain the fluid out. He came promptly to help.

The procedure proved helpful, and later on I had to repeat it several times due to the recurrence of the effusion. I knew that I was not going to be able to stay with her in Baghdad. While I was helping with her breathing, I was putting together a few pieces of furniture, including the steamer trunk, a mattress, a comfortable chair, lots of books, some kitchen utensils, and an Aladdin lamp. My good friend told me that he would continue to do the paracentesis and help my mother in my absence. Even now, I am still overcome with grief as I write about one of the saddest times in my life.

Knowing he was there in my absence when I left for the new job did give me a sense of peace at a difficult time. I found that my new home had been cleaned and a partition installed between a bedroom and the exam room. I was not pleased about the size of either room but there was no alternative.

Behind my room and the exam room there was a small toilet room. The toilet was what in our part of the world, is called a Turkish toilet. It was no more than a hole in the ground which allows the person to squat astride it to do his thing. The hole leads to a cistern or what is called a septic tank, which was still definitely better than going out to do one's job in the wilderness. Behind the rooms and the toilet there was a large piece of bare land fenced in with a high wall that served as a recreation area.

The clinic had a vigorous start as if the people had been anxiously waiting for a doctor to arrive; it was the first time they'd had the luxury of medical care. The kind of patients I was seeing in the first few weeks were the simple illnesses such as bronchitis, colds, and fevers of unknown causes. Then the patients came with congestive heart failures, diabetes, tuberculosis, and other more complicated debilitating conditions such as bilharziasis (parasitic infection of the bladder), Ankylostomas (parasitic infection of the small intestine), etc. They came walking, riding their donkeys, and when available, by cars.

My meetings with the sheikh were semi-regular. It was about once every two or three weeks. Usually, he expected me to give him an injection of something. At that time liver extract injections were touted as a very powerful tonic which was asked for by anyone who felt the need for more vigor and more energy. Testosterone was new on the market and was more likely to help those older people seeking a remedy for their sagging sexual health. (We were not in the era of Cialis or Viagra yet.) He and I developed a genuinely close relationship based on his feeling that he and his tribe were in better medical hands than before and my feeling that I could learn from this wise man about the history and politics of tribal life.

As much as I dreaded my presence in that area at the beginning, I started to enjoy my life with these simple folks. My clinic was always full of mothers covered from top to bottom with their *abayas*, which is like a long black cloak. They arrived with their toddlers and their babies as soon as I opened the clinic door. For them it was a place to go. They sat in the waiting room as if this were a park. Before long the men came and waited outside as they discussed what was important to them.

I hired a man to help with the crowd and with the cleaning, and to keep the chattering people from disrupting my work. One day he asked me if I wanted his wife to cook lunch for me. He said that she was a good cook. I had been surviving on bread bought from a neighbor with boiled eggs or cheese and some canned meats that I brought from Baghdad every time I went home.

The village had no grocery store in the real sense of the word. There was one small dingy-looking shop. It sold tobacco, canned foods, cigarettes and occasionally some fruits and vegetables. Food in a small isolated village is very simple. Bread or rice is the staple food. Meat is seldom eaten unless someone slaughters a sheep for a special occasion. In that area, fish was easy to get, and the people caught the fish for themselves. Chicken was more available. But chickens produce eggs which are more highly coveted as they can serve the family's needs in more ways than chicken. After I started eating my helper's cooking, I often found those lunches unappetizing. I encouraged him to buy some chickens and keep them in their backyard for my and his family's use, and I also went back to the fresh bread that his wife baked very nicely.

Bathing was a problem. In the first two weeks, I had to wade gingerly into the river very early in the morning before the women went out to bring water in for their families. Later, my helper and I positioned a large tank on top of a homemade scaffold from which I could siphon water for a shower. In the evening, I used my Aladdin which gave me a bright light to read. I also had a battery run the radio for news and music. And so went my life in the service of the government during the third year.

Had it not been for my mother's deteriorating health I would have considered that year the most picturesque and romantic of my five years of medical service. Every week I made the trip in my Mercedes to Baghdad to see Mom and help in taking care of her. I was aware by the first week in July of 1958 that my mother did not have more than a couple of weeks to live. Her intake of food was very poor, and her breathing required regular paracentesis. Our lives were in disarray and agony.

On the 14th of July, 1958, our lives changed drastically and permanently in Iraq. General ʿAbdul al-Karīm Qāsim, a military commander walked with all the battalions at his command into Baghdad occupying the main government facilities. His forces occupied the Royal Palace and killed the king and his whole family, dragging some of them in the streets of Baghdad as a vicious sign of defiance and disregard of all civilized protocols.

The coup had not been anticipated by anyone in the secret service or other divisions of the military who effectually surrendered without much resistance. Within a few days, the government was militarized with all important positions occupied by high-ranking military personnel lacking experience in running a government.

Prime Minister Nuri Al-Said went into hiding but was captured trying to escape in woman's garb with all the usual covers. He was shot dead and his body was dragged in the streets of Baghdad. There were various speculations as to who was behind the coup. As far as the people understood, the reason for the coup was the belief by the military that the ruling government was corrupt and controlled by the British colonialists. The prime minister, the king, and most of the parliament were accused of being lackeys of the British.

Some of the speculators thought that the general was a communist, but that thought was wiped out completely when he gave a speech in one of the largest Catholic churches threatening the communists who were prohibited from politics in Iraq, that he would destroy them if they interfered with people's lives or their faiths. He admonished them to obey the military rules. He also spoke to the people of Iraq to come to him if they felt they were being persecuted or threatened by any organization. After that famous speech, people began to warm up to his rule and forgive him for the gruesome bloodshed that the military perpetrated. One of the gains for the people was the freedom of religious beliefs for the minorities.

# The Man from Baghdad

After about a month, life returned to some semblance of normality. The government started to function albeit with some restrictions. The bookstores were flooded with books which were forbidden reading. Relationship with Russia, which had been non-existent, was restored. We started to receive "specialists" in various fields from Russia. There were agricultural, economic, political and even medical specialists. Most of the educated people in the country were not very trusting of this change but were somewhat reassured by the general's assurances.

It was fifteen days after the start of the revolution that my mother's condition became alarming. I needed to go to Baghdad to be with my family. We were almost sure that she was in her final days. Travelling was difficult due to military checkpoints. I had no one to cover for me. I needed more than a weekend. I decided to be assertive, called the Ministry of Health and asked to speak to the minister. The operator told me that he was not taking calls. I told him that I have a serious emergency. The minister was familiar with my name as he was a doctor who graduated a few years before me. After a few minutes he was on the line. He was obviously in an irritable mood. "What is the emergency, Doctor?"

I was rather nervous as I explained to him that I needed two weeks off due to the imminent demise of my mother, and that I will have to leave my clinic without coverage.

He said, "Go ahead, but if I don't get proof that your mother is dying, you will face a military tribunal."

As soon as I put the phone down, I left for Baghdad.

My mother was slipping in and out of consciousness when I arrived. I kept sitting her up to breathe and putting her down to rest. She was aware of all of us standing there. She started crying and asked to kiss my sisters, then my brother and I, and finally my father, who was falling apart. She died a few hours later.

Everything changed after that moment. It was like the thread of a worry bead broke and all the beads scattered on the floor. She was our string that bound us together. After the funeral I made copies of the obituaries from three newspapers and took them personally to the minister. His secretary called him and asked if he would see me. He opened the door, shook my hand and expressed his condolences. He appeared to have read the obituary earlier. I gave him my copies saying these are for the record.

Mother had dealt with much sadness in her life. I think she probably went to visit her family only three or four times in thirty-two years. My father's income was barely enough for our needs so she could not visit her sisters and brothers frequently. The untimely death of her first child was a devastating loss that she never overcame. Despite her sadness, she gave each of us, including my dad, a lot of love and caring. She had endured the long struggle with my sister Nadia who was very reclusive and often oppositional. (It was not until many years later that we realized that Nadia was fighting a very serious mental illness.)

At the age of fifty-eight Mother had been diagnosed with cancer of the breast. For the next four years she suffered from the cancer, as well as the ill effects of the various therapies she received.

After her death, my father stopped going out except to go to work. He declined visits to his friends, even his brother and sister. He was driven in the morning to work and was driven back home at 1 o'clock in the afternoon. He was very depressed. After work he would sit and stare into the distance. His younger brother used to come and visit him once a week but could not engage him in a decent conversation. This condition lasted about two years before he began to show some interest in things. For us, the younger generation, this was a terrible time dealing with and worrying about him, as well as dealing with our own grief.

I went back to work after the two weeks. The patients were happy to see me back and the clinic was getting more and more busy. About two months after the start of the revolution, a government car stopped in front of the clinic and the men standing outside waiting for their turn to see me came in to say that there is an important man coming to visit. I walked outside, and lo and behold, the minister of health was chatting with the patients. I was worried that something bad had happened. He smiled and complimented me on the reports he was getting from the patients. I asked him into my small exam room. He told me that he had received great reports from the sheikh and the government workers about the clinic.

He informed me that there was an opening in a much larger nearby hospital that served a wider area that had been neglected for a while and they needed someone like me to go and clean up the mess. The town had a twenty-four-bed hospital, an outpatient clinic and a nice adjoining house for the doctor. I was dismayed at first glance and told him that I was happy where I was, and I liked the people that I was serving. They might feel that I was abandoning them; and what about the sheikh?

He said he would talk to the sheikh next. He would send him a new graduate and wanted me with my experience to go to Shahraban (now called Muqdadiyah). He said that I should receive the order in a couple of days. He wanted me to start work the first week of December.

During the last two months in the village I spent all my evenings reading. Because of the freedom we were enjoying I read much of Karl Marx's writings, classical Russian literature, a great deal of Arabic literature, and I reviewed my French and German, both of which I studied during my military years. I was sad that I was going to lose my spare time due to the ten-hour-a-day schedule that was going to be necessary in my new job. But I was a government employee and I had to obey orders.

By the next morning, the news of my departure had spread in the village and I had to deal with a near riot by the people. The women were crying. They and their children had a great year of medical care. The men were angry and swearing at the callousness of the revolution, etc. The sheikh came and thanked me for the good work that I had done for him, his family and his tribe, and wished me good luck in my new life. In his wisdom he realized that in these days of the revolution sheikhs were no longer as important or influential in the eyes of the government.

# The Man from Baghdad

I started my new job a month later. I knew that I was going to need Peter, my old assistant/cook/secretary. I went back home and asked him if he was interested in another year of adventures. He was agreeable. We took what we needed and headed to Shahraban. We had a big comfortable house. There were shops and groceries, and even a kebab restaurant. However, the hospital was a mess; dirty, no meds for the patients, no training for the staff, and most importantly no caring physician. The doctor whom I replaced spent most of his time in his private office leaving the medical care of the people to the untrained staff. Apparently, the people complained to the Ministry of Health and he was removed from his job.

For one hour every morning, my staff and I had a tutorial with a question-and-answer routine. The rounds in the hospital with the staff came next. Besides seeing the patients, we inspected the hygiene and cleanliness of the facility, the beds and covers and the clothes the patients were wearing. The instruments had to be autoclaved properly. One of the nurses was responsible for ordering meds from the health ministry. Within a month the hospital and outpatient clinic were functioning.

I was the only doctor at the hospital, but there were two doctors in town practicing privately, including the one who was fired from the hospital job before my arrival. I had two nurses, three nurse assistants, and some servants to clean and keep order in the outpatient clinic. One wonders how we managed at that time without secretaries. We had to do things ourselves, and the nursing staff sometimes did what secretaries do now.

Work in this community was brisk and the patients were a bit more sophisticated. There were teachers, housewives of military personal, government employees, and other people one meets in a larger town. They had more experience with what the clinic should look like and how it should function. I was beginning to realize that the government was gradually setting me up for "greater things."

Shahraban's population was about five to six thousand. It was built alongside a highway that goes northwest toward Iran and was about an hour's drive from Mandali where forty years earlier my father had been exiled by the Turkish authorities. My father used to tell us about the months he spent in that town after his death sentence was commuted and exile was ordered.

The revolution, which I mentioned earlier, started from a sprawling barrack not too far away from this town, which explained why a large number of military families were getting their medical care from us. We were also seeing patients who spoke Persian due to our proximity to the Iranian border.

As the hospital began to function, patients who had been going to private doctors started to seek care from our outpatient service. It was a very invigorating job. I was learning a lot and getting to know the people and their medical needs and how to provide them with care. Again, this was a rural hospital and we could only provide general medicine, pediatric care, and minor surgery. All serious conditions that required surgeons, gynecologists, cardiologist, etc., were referred to Baghdad.

# The Man from Baghdad

My personal life in that town was not very exciting, however; in fact, it was basically mundane, though it did increase my experience and ability to deal with people. I did not come across any interesting events there. I had the opportunity to visit my family almost every weekend. Farouq and my two sisters were working and taking care of Dad and the house. My father was still quite withdrawn; going home was also not very exciting at that time.

Around that time, I had met a girl who worked as a nurse in a Baghdad hospital where I used to visit a colleague on my trips to Baghdad. From the moment we met outside her workplace, I was faced with the same dilemma as I had with my first girlfriend. She too was Muslim. She was about twenty-three and single. She expressed a desire to see me from time to time with the same conditions as before.

I was twenty-eight and single, living and working in areas where I was unlikely to meet an eligible Christian girl. Christians in Iraq lived in three or four large cities in the country, but I was lonely. Therefore, I yielded to another temptation—a relationship that was not going anywhere. But it was nice to come home to Baghdad to spend a few hours with a young lady who was intelligent, cheerful and sociable.

Naturally, we had to be very cautious. Her father was deceased, and because her mother worked during the day, she often invited me to her home for a cup of coffee and cake. This romance ended the same way the first one did. She told me that her mother's family found her a gentleman who was interested in marrying her. Once again, I went through the same heartache of separation, but that time I'd been anticipating the loss. We had talked about it and accepted the possibility. Neither she nor I was able or willing to change our religions due to society's taboos.

It was during that time that I began to ponder about my medical future. I was interested in the field of internal medicine. I had already practiced it for four years and one year in the army. I talked with colleagues who had already acquired a specialty in a foreign country, and I looked at what the government might need in the field of medicine and reached the conclusion that internal medicine was it. I was going to concentrate on that field.

Near the end of 1959, I was informed by the minister of health that I was to be transferred to a large hospital in the central part of Iraq, to be the head of the medical department at The Middle Euphrates Hospital. It was located near a very religious city in Iraq called Kufa.

I was stunned by the sudden elevation in responsibility that this change engendered. Although it was a sign of confidence on the part of the ministry of health, I felt a bit overwhelmed to become responsible for a medical department with some forty inpatient beds and an intense outpatient clinic. It was a very large hospital that had acted as a regional tertiary hospital between Baghdad and Basra, which is the third largest city in Iraq, located in the southernmost part of Iraq. There were a number of specialty departments including obstetrics and gynecology, ear nose and throat, internal medicine, urology, and surgery. It was scary to think about, but I had to obey orders and I was getting closer to the end of my responsibility to the government: one more year.

My departure from the last town was not memorable. I did enjoy and learn from my experience, but overall, my life in Shahraban was isolated and lonely. My servant was also bored. He thought the people there were not as sociable and friendly as in Musayab. But my family was beginning to find their own interests and my mother who had looked forward to my visits was gone. My visits to Baghdad were not rejuvenating and not exciting.

My trips to the family became shorter and farther between.

The region of the new hospital was located close to a highly religious area for the Shia Sect of Islam, thousands of people came to visit various shrines in Kufa and Nejaf. Many of them came from neighboring countries like Iran, Saudi Arabia and Kuwait. Many came and stayed after their pilgrimage. Many of the poor pilgrims welcomed the opportunity of seeking free medical care in that newly built hospital.

I was assigned to live in a newly built house which I shared with two other doctors. There were three of these houses built in a row and meant for the newly appointed physicians. I was also informed that the hospital was expecting four doctors from Russia to be sent to train and help the Iraqi doctors. This was the time when Iraq was on very good relations with the Soviets. This cooperation gave birth to the suspicion that the leaders of the revolution were steering away from the West, especially England, and cozying up to Russia. During this period, there was an attempt on the president's life. It was a serious harbinger—the president and his trusted advisers were keenly aware that the West was not happy about the turn of events.

At the end of the year, I moved to my fifth assignment. I was ready to serve the last year of my commitment before I started the next phase of my life. I found the house as described, very satisfactory, the hospital in good shape and living amenities in town more abundant than in my previous assignments. Although Kufa was the nearest city to the hospital, Nejaf was a more populous city. It was about a twenty-minute drive from my house. I opened my private office in Nejaf, even though there were many private doctors with various specialties already there.

Nejaf is venerated by the Islamic world, especially the Shia Sect as the place where Ali ibn Abi Talib, the cousin of the prophet Muhammad, was buried. Interestingly, Ali wanted his grave to remain secret lest it would be desecrated. It is said that it so stayed until the Caliph Harun al-Rashid, many years later while on a deer hunting trip, stumbled on it and asked for a mausoleum to be built there. A lot of religious institutions were built around this grave which itself developed into the magnificent Mosque of 'Ali. The mosque grew into a singularly magnificent shrine decorated with small cut mirrors and precious stones on the inside walls and dome. It was very interesting for me as a Christian to visit the mosque courtesy of one of the religious *imams* whom I befriended. Subsequently, I learned how to visit with my friends in the Holy Place without a companion by not attracting attention to myself.

# The Man from Baghdad

A very famous and holy place around Nejaf is the cemetery which I was told was the largest in the world. Acres upon acres, if not more, one can see headstones of millions of Shias who were buried there to be close to the holy imam. They were brought by their families at great cost from all over the world. All those who are buried there believed that they will rise with the imam on judgement day. In addition, Al-Husayn, the son of Ali was buried in the area.

For the first time in my life I began to be interested in the history of Islam in more depth than our studies in high school had provided. I was spending more time with the local people who, in general, were very well read in the philosophy and jurisprudence of their religion. I met many scholars, from whom I got to understand some of the different streams of thoughts that they immersed themselves in, and how about one thousand, four hundred and fifty years before, Kufa, a close neighbor of Nejaf, was considered a very quarrelsome and murderous troublemaker city in the early history of Islam. It was in this area that Ali ibn Abi Talib (the prophet's cousin) was assassinated. Later on, his son Al-Husayn and his whole family and companions were massacred.

The work was not as complicated in the hospital. I did not have to supervise my colleagues. We had all trained in the same school. Problems began to emerge with the four Russian doctors.

In the first place, they spoke not a word of Arabic. Of course, neither the patients nor we doctors spoke any Russian. To be fair to the Russian authorities who sent them, they also sent an interpreter to facilitate our interaction. They spoke a few English words, but the interpreter who was a beautiful twenty-two-year-old blond Russian woman found herself running from one doctor to the other trying to help them understand the complaints of the patients as well as to help the patients understand the instructions of the doctors. Their group consisted of a gynecologist, an ear, nose and throat specialist, an internist and a surgeon. The interpreter spoke English, Arabic, Azerbaijani, Persian, and of course Russian. Even though she was not familiar with colloquial Arabic she made an effort to learn. She had graduated from the University of Moscow, the Foreign Languages School.

She became friendly with my staff and me to the point that in the afternoon break she would come to the doctors' house and we would drink tea or coffee and sit and talk. We talked about Russia as it was at that time, and also about the Arabic countries and their history.

The female gynecologist whom we suspected was a KGB spy watched whoever talked to this girl. I am ashamed that I forgot her name. One evening she walked, from her neighboring home in the dark to our house and told me that the KGB lady told her that she was not acting in an acceptable manner and was getting too close to the locals. She was asked to pack her belongings because a car from the Russian Embassy would be picking her up in the early morning to send her back to Russia.

I was angry and upset about being left with four doctors who would be useless without an interpreter. I also worried about this girl's future after she told me that she may face discipline, or jail, when she got back home. I gave her my father's address and phone number in Baghdad in case she needed a place to stay. I woke up early in the morning when I heard a car stopping by the Russian's door and then I saw her leave.

My father called me two days later and said that a stunningly beautiful girl came to our house in a chauffeured car and left me a Russian/English dictionary with a letter. The letter was a sad one about how much she loved being with us, thanking us for our friendship, and still expressing anxiety about her future. Khrushchev was the chairman of the USSR at that time.

Not only was that experience very demoralizing for my staff and me, but it added to the problems we were having with the Russian delegation that was supposed to be training us. After exchanging stories about medical education in Russia and Iraq, we found that medical education in Russia at that time was for four years only as compared to six years in Iraq, and in my case, it was actually seven years. Their experience was so meager that my staff and all other Iraqi doctors were alerted to follow the Russian colleagues from case to case to check on their diagnosis and treatment as well as their surgical work. After what happened to our interpreter, we had a good understanding of how life must have been in Russia.

The spring of that year I started thinking more seriously of specializing in internal medicine. England at that time was the place to go. In the first place, we would be trained by British professors, and secondly, the school system was very similar to ours. In addition, the government only paid for specialization in England because it was cheaper and closer in case a student needed to return. I made an appointment with the minister of health.

The new minister was a friend of mine and had a good idea about my work in the previous four-and-a-half years. He and I talked about my plan and he told me that he would get back to me after finding out more about the availabilities of medical scholarships. The system in Iraq for education was the same as in some other countries after high school. If a student has the grades or qualifications, as well as the motivation, he could get a specialization scholarship with all reasonable expenses paid if there is a need in the country for that field. Payback was the same as in my previous arrangement with the government. One had to serve five years in his field where the need exists.

The response from the minister was disappointing. There was no need for internal medicine at that time. There was, however, a need for psychiatry. At that time, having practiced internal medicine for five years, I felt so close to the subject that I knew I would make a good internist. On the other hand, I remembered that I had been interested in psychiatry when I was in medical school.

I decided to take that offer with the idea that if I didn't like the courses, I would try and change to internal medicine somehow. Later on, when I was in England, I decided I did not have to change. I was settled as far as my future education was concerned. I had to get my application and degrees ready and the government was going to take care of all the arrangements. I immersed myself in my work at the hospital with the excitement of going to England always on my mind.

It was around that period that another mega traumatic event occurred in my life. One afternoon, while I was seeing patients in the outpatient department, a knock on the door interrupted me and the door opened. My brother Farouq stood there. It was not like my brother to show up at my place of work without notice. I was shocked to see him. His appearance portended Bad News. I knew he had traveled two hours to tell me about the problem face to face. I thought that my father had died, or some terrible catastrophe had taken place. I felt the blood drain from my face; I was speechless and lightheaded. He told me to put my jacket on so I could go with him immediately to Baghdad.

"I can't just leave; I still have patients to see," I said to him.

"Our sister Nadia took an overdose of medications and is in the hospital, comatose. We fear she is dying," he replied. He came to drive me because he knew that I would not have been able to drive in my state of shock.

I asked one of my doctors to see the rest of the patients and we headed to Baghdad. Nadia was a very complicated girl. She was a great concern to all of us. Especially to Mom, who had worried that Nadia had no friends or companions to talk with about her feelings. When Mom had attempted to reach out to Nadia, she was repeatedly rebuffed with anger.

I always tried to understand her mood changes, but they were inscrutable. She was inclined to be very withdrawn and asocial. On the other hand, I was always sure that Nadia was the most intelligent of all of us kids with a creative and perceptive mind. She loved decorating the new house which we had built in 1955. In addition, her fascination with the history of Western Europe was one of her main interests. She spoke French and English fluently, and Arabic of course.

We arrived at the nun's hospital and found Nadia still comatose. My father looked totally demoralized, and my younger sister Ameera was sitting in a corner crying quietly, terrified as to what was going to happen to her older sister who was like a mother substitute to her. I examined Nadia carefully and checked her vital signs and nerve reflexes and found that she was not in imminent danger.

The neurologist, Dr. Jack Abboodi, came later and decided to give her a stimulant which was a popular drug at that time. The drug was repeated through the night. By morning she began to stir and by evening she was responsive to our questions. I reassured my father and sister that Nadia was going to make it and assured Farouq that I would be available.

The next day Farouq drove me back to my job, I was an emotional wreck. My sister was very dear to me even if I could not always understand her thoughts and her feelings, nor for that matter, her wishes and dreams. At one time she wanted to go to Switzerland and study costume design. She was very interested in fashions and drew dress designs that she had tailored for her wear. She filled tens of pages of drawings of her designs that were very appealing and promising, but made no effort to make arrangements or plans to send them to support applications to fashion schools abroad.

She was engaged to a Belgian gentleman whom she met at work. Her fiancé had been with her night and day when she was struggling for her life in the hospital. He was mystified about her event, not knowing what it meant and how it was going to affect their relationship.

This incident with Nadia was a terrible experience for all of us. She remained quieter and more withdrawn; she refused to talk about her overdose. She went to see our family physician a couple of times but refused to talk about what she tried to do. She managed to go back to her job at the Belgian engineering company without revealing to anyone *anything* about her feelings or the reasons behind her attempt. I asked her if she felt trapped in the relationship with her fiancé, but she told me that she did not know why she did what she did.

A year later, when I began studying psychiatry in England, I revisited that incident trying to understand the whys and wherefores of what happened and with my new-found knowledge I finally realized that all her life she felt that she was misunderstood by all of us. She had always been dealing with an insidious case of schizophrenia. There were moments when her symptoms abated and moments when she was dealing with her fears and her demons.

It was my opinion then that her engagement and the prospect of marriage and leaving her security at home may have precipitated that serious suicide attempt. Despite her obvious lack of a warm relationship with the family, she was afraid to risk leaving her home.

Nadia's overdose occurred in the spring of 1959. She married in the spring of 1960.

Widad Bazzoui's siblings in 1958:

Nadia, Farouq, and Ameera.

## Chapter Six

# Onward to England

In August 1960, I flew to London to start my studies in psychiatry at the Maudsley Hospital. By the time I took to the air, I was resigned to some extent that the rest of the family was more settled. My father was still working. Nadia was a newlywed and recovered—at least on the surface. She was working and doing her share, even though we never knew what really drove her to attempt suicide. Ameera, the baby of the family, and the most genuine and compassionate of all of us, had begun a new job at the Swiss Embassy. She was beginning to feel grown up and more confident. Farouq was enjoying himself, having been making good money through the construction contracts he was supervising with his partners.

The flight was long, about eight hours with a stop in Istanbul. When I was in the air, I started worrying about how I would manage living in London. I began to dwell on how I was going to face for the first time in my life the challenge of living so far away from family and friends.

My anxiety mounted when I took the train for London. However, everything turned out to be simpler than I expected. While at the airport, I was given the names of several hotels that cater to newcomers and I struck good luck when I arrived at the first hotel and found out that the owners were from Baghdad.

They had apparently left Iraq in the late forties when the Jewish minority in Iraq was beginning to leave for Israel. The hotel owner was not only from Baghdad, but he knew my father and welcomed me warmly, asking about various people who were known to both our families. I decided to stay there for a few weeks until I was able to navigate in London, find the least expensive places to eat and live. I also had to learn the cheapest and shortest way to get daily to the Maudsley Hospital where my training was to take place.

London in the Sixties was a remarkable place to live. England had not yet been overshadowed by hordes of foreigners changing its English nature to a mishmash of nationalities, languages, and colors. There was a variety of opportunities to explore, and learn, and yet one could feel the freedom to say and do, as one could not in the Middle East. There were endless varieties of food, entertainment, museums and classical music centers. London was still British. Since then I have visited London many times and I can't help noticing the international chaos that exists.

After four weeks, I moved to a nice small room in an apartment that belonged to an elderly German lady who made it clear that she was particular about cleanliness, noise, and the hours that I intended to come home. She told me ten p.m. was my limit. That was later changed to midnight after I gained her trust. The place was very close to the *young* activity on Queens Way. Although I was not a night owl, I could not refrain from immersing myself in the various activities such as concerts, museums, etc. While there, I renewed my relationship with colleagues with whom I graduated from medical school. They were there studying different specialties in medicine.

Of course, I was on a strict monthly budget. I was on a scholarship from the government of Iraq from which I received sixty British pounds a month, (equivalent today to about one hundred and twenty dollars). I had eight hundred British pounds from the sale of my car, which I saved for an emergency. I had to be very frugal. My room, and later on my apartment, cost me twenty-five pounds a month, leaving only thirty-five pounds to pay for everything else such as clothing, transportation, food and entertainment. An occasional check from my father was always welcome.

I attended the Institute of Psychiatry, which at that time was a part of the University of London. It was a prestigious psychiatric institute. I attended lectures, seminars, and inpatient rounds every day. It was very impressive and at the same time enjoyable. We started promptly at nine a.m. and finished at five p.m., enough time to go home to study, despite the distractions of London nightlife.

Farouq and his beautiful bride, Hasmeek, visited London on their honeymoon, just a few months after my arrival. They were no problem as they both knew London and entertained themselves.

My sister, Ameera, called to tell me she and Farouq had convinced Dad to visit me in London. They had already booked a flight. He was escorted to the airport in Baghdad by his three adult children. I was waiting for him at the airport in London when he arrived. I was very happy to see him.

By that time, about two years after my arrival in England, I had moved to a single-room apartment in West Hampstead, a little out of the center of London. It was more comfortable and more affordable than my first apartment. I booked him in the hotel that belonged to his old friend from Baghdad, where I'd first stayed upon my arrival in London. Dad enjoyed the company of his old friend while I was in classes. He played backgammon in the hotel lobby many afternoons during his visit.

I went over every day after school and took him out to a concert, a show or to dinner. The trip gave us a chance to grow closer and to explore all the important changes in our family.

I took him to the men's shops on Saville Row in London to buy a tailored suit. I couldn't afford one, but I was sure my father could manage it. He chose a fine dark navy wool fabric; he looked like a king when he wore it. It was good to see him smile again.

He managed to learn the area and took long walks exploring the shops and other interesting places. After about a month he had to go back having used all his vacation time. Before returning to Baghdad, he urged me to think about finding a wife and settling down; he said, "It is time, son." He told my siblings that he had a wonderful trip.

The third year I was in England I traveled to Brussels, Belgium, to visit Nadia, who had recently moved there as expected when her husband was transferred back home. She was on the surface pleasant, though guarded and serious. She did not cook but did serve me several cups of tea in her lavish and large apartment that reminded me more of a museum than a home. She spoke of her isolation and the coldness of her in-laws and the Belgium people in general. She did not show any alarming signs of emotional disturbances, though she was obviously not cheerful or light-hearted. But then, she had never exuded happiness before in her life.

At the end of my three years in school, and while I was studying hard for my finals, my cousin Jack arrived and stayed with me in my apartment for two weeks. Fortunately, despite my houseguest, I managed to pass with the higher-ranking students of the class.

Soon after that I applied for a job at Tooting Beck Hospital, a British state hospital where I thought I could get hands–on experience. The job was approved, and I promptly started working. Through this job I gained a lot of experience and new knowledge in the care of patients with chronic mental illness, which I knew I would need in Iraq.

It was there that I experienced my first physical attack by a patient under my care. The patient was my professor's and he asked me to see him instead. No sooner had he entered my office with his wife, then he rushed me and punched me over and over in the face and chest, all the while accusing me of being a C.I.D. agent, an F.B.I. equivalent. I ended up with three broken ribs and lacerations in the face. I always remembered that as a warning at that early stage of my career. Subsequently, despite being careful, I have sustained more physical attacks over the years.

During the time I worked at Tooting Beck, I met a young German girl, Ilse, who was in London to study English. Over the next few months our relationship grew closer and we decided to marry. I knew I was not going to stay in England. Her mother wanted information about my family, my religion and so forth. My father kindly obliged. We were married in a very small service in a Catholic church in London a few weeks before our trip back to Iraq. Those in attendance were her mother, and my friends Gilbert and Aida Toma. My father had sent letters and I had informed Ilse and her mother about what to expect in Iraq, socially, the weather, and the other aspects of life in the Middle East.

In April 1964 we flew to Baghdad.

# Chapter Seven

# Back to Baghdad

Our flight to Baghdad was uneventful with a short layover in Istanbul. My whole family was at the airport to welcome us home. I introduced my new wife, who, still stunned by her first Turkish toilet experience, told them about the hole in the floor at the Ankara Airport women's restroom. At home we were treated to an Iraqi feast. And life gradually settled into a routine.

Soon after I arrived, I started looking for a job, but the ministry of health was already looking for me. I was immediately informed to report to my new position as the assistant director of the Shamma'eya Psychiatric Hospital. Dr. Tariq Hamdi was the medical director until he left to teach at the medical school in Baghdad. Shamma'eya was looked at by the public as a mysterious and scary place where the ill-fated insane patients are sentenced to live their lives, shut away from society.

I was shocked at the condition of the hospital; patients roamed the grounds aimlessly, except for the forensic unit, which was locked. Some were clad, others were not. Some of the more reliable patients were given jobs such as cleaning or helping with the laundry. The others were left to their own devices.

There were few medications. Paraldehyde and Thorazine were almost the only psychiatric medications available, but only a few patients were medicated. The units were unsanitary and crowded. Instead of thirteen hundred patients, which was the official number of beds, we had two thousand. The nursing staff had no training in mental health. The patient's diagnoses were not in keeping with modern criteria.

The forensic unit was a jungle. Doctors never entered for fear of attack. A couple of male nurses, whom the patients had come to fear, or "respect," had that responsibility. The new acting director assigned me the task of organizing the unit. It was a challenge since the medical staff and most of the nursing staff refused to help.

The two male nurses who knew the patients' habits helped me evaluate each unfortunate man, one at a time. Their charts consisted mostly of legal information and it was all we had to start with. A working diagnosis and treatment plan were made with an evaluation of their level of dangerousness. After a few months, the census of that department was reduced from three hundred to two hundred. The unit was cleaned. The patients were given instructions in personal hygiene and the patients thought to be of insignificant risk were moved to open units.

This process was repeated in all the units. After learning the different categories of mental illness, the nursing staff was gradually trained to observe changes in patients, both positive and negative. We had a unit for severe epileptics. We selected the patients who would benefit from regular electric shock treatment to reduce the frequency of seizures. Of course, electric shock was given with no anesthesia. We had none to give.

When I started to work there, I was happy to see my friend, Dr. Fa'ik Odo as we had agreed in England to work together in Iraq, and to bring *this* hospital to British hospital standards. But we soon realized Iraq was not England. Since I did not have a car yet, I was using my father's car or riding with Dr. Odo to and from work.

Every time we needed a prescription for a patient, we had to go to the Ministry of Health to explain the reasons and the uses of the meds. Stelazine was coming out. Tofranil was popular. Mellaril was already in use. Haldol, "Seranace" was being advertised. We needed antibiotics, intravenous fluids, vaccines, etc. In the Iraqi health system, mental illness was at the bottom of the priority scale.

Dr. Felix Georji, a friend of mine, was appointed director of the hospital in 1965. By then we had gone through the main job of sanitizing the hospital, classifying patients, training the staff, and introducing new methods of managing infections, violence and physical problems. He was a very effective director because of his experience with dealing with bureaucracy. He successfully negotiated for more nurses, staff, and medications. This allowed the psychiatrists time to deal more effectively with the patient's medical and psychiatric problems.

It was while all this excitement was going on that I started doing my research and writing my papers. I wrote about the history of our hospital, about psychiatry in Iraq, the attitude and beliefs of the people and the clinical symptomatology of bipolar disorders in Iraq as compared with the western version of the disease. I used my private patients to collect the data. I felt that the patients who had not received treatment (virgin patients) provided an unbiased sample to work with psychologists and psychiatrists to validate my observations.

In the second year of my work at Shamma'eya, we were faced with sudden deaths in different wards. The dead were young healthy males who had not complained of physical illness. It was mystifying and frightening. I reported the deaths to the Ministry of Health. Autopsies were done and the reports came back negative for physical causes. The only thing the four deceased had in common was they were all taking the same new anti-psychotic medication, Mellaril.

I wrote to the pharmaceutical company and informed them of my suspicion that their new anti-psychotic medication had caused these four men to have cardiac arrests. The pharmaceutical company never responded to my letter. We limited the dosage of that anti-psychotic medication to no more than 100 mg per day and we had no more sudden deaths. Several years later that pharmaceutical company issued a warning (Black Box) about the prolongation of the RST interval in the heart leading to sudden death. Even though we did not get recognition for our discovery, a psychiatrist in a third-world country brought the risk to the attention of a pharmaceutical giant.

The next year, during morning report one day, a nurse reported that a number of patients in another unit had fallen ill with severe diarrhea. I investigated and found that these were not simple cases of diarrhea. It was cholera. I found two of the patients fighting for their lives. They had had visitors from a distant area a few days earlier. At that time, Iran had declared they had cases of cholera in their country. The director of the hospital asked me to manage the situation because of my background in internal medicine.

Again, we had no antibiotics, no intravenous fluids, and the nursing staff was not trained in taking care of communicable diseases. We quarantined the hospital and isolated the units from each other. All staff members were vaccinated and the patients soon after. All direct staff was quarantined with the patients. I called the minister of health and told him I was certain on clinical grounds we were dealing with cholera. He told me there was no cholera in Iraq. Two days later, lab tests proved my diagnoses correct. We had one hundred and four cases and lost six or seven patients. I stayed at the hospital for a week. I was afraid to leave my patients, and also afraid of infecting my wife and baby.

The epidemic soon hit the rest of the country. Two months after Iraq was declared clear of cholera, representatives of W.H.O. (World Health Organization) applauded the staff of the hospital for their dedication in stopping the spread of the disease with such a low mortality count. The minister of health sent me a letter thanking me for my role in controlling the epidemic in the hospital. I still have the letter.

Psychiatry at that time was beginning to be recognized by other medical disciplines, and patients were being referred to private psychiatrists. I saw patients in my private office from about four in the afternoon until eight or nine at night. Most of my colleagues also saw patients in their private offices during the evenings. Sometimes I gave electric shock treatments in my office. As stated before, we had no anesthesia or muscle relaxants at that time.

Meanwhile, adjusting to married life in Baghdad was difficult for my German wife and me. We lived with my father in his large home, as did my brother and his wife, as well as my younger sister. My sister-in-law was very eager to help my German wife adjust to the Arabic customs, traditions and cultural restrictions in women's lives in Iraq. My wife had asked many questions about life in Iraq before our marriage. She accepted that she would have to adjust to our culture. Many graduates who studied abroad came back with western spouses who made the transition very well.

It became obvious that she was having a great deal of difficulty accepting the cultural boundaries in our society. She resented my sister–in-law's recommendations and felt those were attempts on the part of my sister-in-law to control her. Not only did this situation become a source of hostility on the part of my wife toward the in-laws, but it began to affect my relationship with my family and with her. She found the restrictions unacceptable even though she and I had talked about them repeatedly before our marriage.

To reduce the friction between the two women, I decided to rent a house next to my father and move out. When I talk about my father's house, I have to explain that I had invested quite significantly in that house before going to England. In a sense it was partly my house too. Be that as it may, I did not want my father to be exposed to the tension between the two women.

Things settled somewhat with distance between the two ladies, but not enough, so a more drastic move was needed. We had to move a little further from my family to reduce the friction. This proved to be a reasonable, but temporary, solution.

A few weeks after my return to Baghdad, my brother called in the late evening to tell me that Dad was sick and had severe pain in his stomach area. I rushed to his house and found my father in very bad shape. After examining him, I felt that he was having intermittent gallbladder colic, which he had had before.

There was something else that worried me, and that was his diabetes which we could not test daily at home at that time. His heart was regular, and his blood pressure was normal. In addition, the pain was not in the chest and it was intermittent and not radiating to the arm, so I was almost sure it was not the heart.

I called his family physician and asked for guidance. He also thought it was not the heart. He suggested a small dose of morphine to relieve the pain, which I did. He asked me to bring him to the hospital as early in the morning as possible for further evaluation and treatment. It was about eleven at night by then. I called my wife to tell her about the situation and told her that I was sleeping in my father's house for the night.

His heart apparently was either at the base of the problem or it was the gall bladder that put stress on his heart, and both his family physician and I were sidetracked by his history of gall bladder problems and missed the real problem. His pain in the abdomen was actually coronary pain.

At four o'clock in the morning, he woke up and told me that his pain was worse, and I called for the ambulance. While we were transferring him to the ambulance, he became confused and started thrashing around. As much as I tried to allay his fears, I could not reach him as he was totally delirious. He died before the ambulance even started for the hospital.

My mind was suddenly numb. I could not comprehend how someone can pass from a state of living to the state of death in such a split second. At the same time, I began to feel the enormity of my loss. My father had been the mainstay in my life.

When he died, as the custom in Iraq goes, we laid him on a bed in the living room, not having funeral homes at that time. The funeral was arranged for the following day. We had to lay him on ice, to allow the family and close friends to say farewell to the deceased. There was no refrigeration at that time. In the morning, by the time the hearse arrived, there were about one hundred and fifty cars parked around the street waiting to take him to church and then the cemetery. At the cemetery, I suddenly felt the panic of being totally alone.

Planning a funeral was a very painful and stressful task. All the members of the extended family participated in making the arrangements. After the burial, all family members, friends, the clergy, and coworkers, etc., came to the family home to share the grief, and participate in the solemn occasion.

The Christians recite a short prayer for the deceased upon arrival to the house and repeat it as they depart. The Muslim neighbors, friends and coworkers offer a special prayer called Al Fātiḥah (the opening prayer of the Quran). Black coffee was served as a sign of respect and sorrow. Smoking was encouraged and cigarettes were offered by the bereaved.

This intense grieving ritual started in the morning by nine with the last mourners departing around nine at night. This continues for three days. The process is re-peated on the fortieth day after the death, fortunately for only one day. During those days, people brought a variety of foods to nourish the bereaved, and those of the extended family and friends who wished to partake of that. Wives, sisters and daughters must wear black. In those days it was an unwritten law to wear black for a year, but in recent years, society has become more relaxed.

When my mother passed away, I was overwhelmed with sorrow and I missed her love, her sense of humor and tenderness. But I had not felt the fear and desolation that my father's death caused.

My father's death was a tragic loss for me; he'd been my rock that I leaned on for the many changes in my life. The memories of his recent trip to London while I was still in training only added to my pain and grief. His quiet and pensive way of dealing with everyday problems was my guide to follow. His love and support for all of us was unwavering. But as everyone who has suffered the loss of someone so dear, I somehow managed to go on.

Then in 1967, my friend and colleague, Dr. Fa'ik Odo, started complaining of dyspeptic discomfort. He tried to treat himself the best he could, with no change. His family physician referred him for x-rays. Tragically, he was diagnosed with stomach cancer. That good and kind doctor began chemo and radiation treatments. When I left Iraq in 1968, I received my last letter from my friend. He said goodbye to me and to his dreams. This good and kind man was taken from us in the prime of his life when he still had so much good to offer to the world.

I remember pondering the circle of life as I still grieved for my father and felt outrage for the loss of my friend, but just a few short months later I would feel such joy with the birth of my first child.

My daughter Reem was born five months after my father passed away. My beautiful baby girl was born prematurely by cesarean due to an attempt by the obstetrician to turn her from breech position. I wrapped her in cotton and transported her in my VW that had no air conditioning in one-hundred-ten-degree heat to a pediatric hospital five miles away. She weighed four pounds, three-and-half ounces. She survived well and grew into a beautiful, intelligent girl.

Reem and Ban Bazzoui in 1973.

Ban and Reem Bazzoui in 1977.

Bazzoui family visits Baghdad, 1978.

## Chapter Eight

# Leaving Iraq

I never considered leaving Iraq while my father was alive. But after that, I began to think of leaving Iraq for the USA to expand my knowledge and possibly obtain an academic position in psychiatry. I had been working in the same hospital since I returned from England. It had already been four years. Working with chronically mentally ill patients is not very stimulating. I was successful in my private practice, working four hours in the evenings, six days a week. But I wanted more academic work.

About that time, I applied to my alma mater, the Iraqi Royal Medical College, for an academic position in the Department of Neurology/Psychiatry. In addition, I had published two research papers in the famous British *Journal of Psychiatry*. I had upgraded the system of care at my neglected hospital, and successfully handled an epidemic of cholera at the hospital.

I also had my letter from the World Health Organization for my work with the cholera outbreak. In addition,

I'd been teaching nurses and general practitioners about psychiatry. I felt I was eminently qualified, so, I applied for the position. I met with the head of the department who was an old friend. He apologized and told me the department did not have the funds to hire another psychiatrist.

Two months later the university department found money to hire a young doctor with no experience, but he belonged to the majority faith. That prompted me to consider looking elsewhere for my next career step.

I knew the USA was recruiting doctors from outside the country. The US government had changed visa regulations to facilitate this project, which also included other scientists. I applied to a number of openings and received acceptance from the Missouri Mental Health Center in Columbia, Missouri. I had passed the ECFMG exam, a must credential to qualify as a medical doctor in the United States.

In 1966 I took my young daughter, Reem, and my wife to visit her family in Germany, and then we drove to Belgium. When we arrived in Brussels, Nadia showed no indication that she wanted us to stay in her large, beautiful apartment. She did not even invite us to see it. We did not want to intrude. She and her husband joined us for dinner at our hotel. Nadia was polite but guarded, and a bit withdrawn. She did not indicate any interest or happiness at meeting my family or seem to appreciate that we had come so far to visit her. Hasmeek and Farouq had a similar experience when they had visited her a year earlier with their two young children.

My wife, who had remained unhappy during her time in Iraq, was very agreeable to the idea of moving to the US. She had never adjusted to Iraq, its culture, and especially not to my family. We had moved three times, each time to better and bigger homes. Despite the fact that there were a number of German families whom we befriended, she had no real friends, which was why we thought going to America would be a good idea.

I informed my family of my plans. In order to leave Iraq, a physician needed a special reason because doctors were leaving and not coming back. I applied for sick leave to go to England for surgical treatment of a cervical prolapsed disc. I was given two months of sick leave. I started preparing my colleagues and my patients that I was leaving for an unknown period of time to have an operation on my neck.

It appears that someone informed the secret service that I was leaving Iraq for good. That was a red flag, and I was henceforth considered a suspicious person who planned to abandon his country. I noticed that I was being followed at times and told my brother. Farouq was well known by the authorities because of his construction company's large government contracts. He told me that we should go talk to the secret service director whom he said was a friend of his.

The director was friendly and respectful. He called his assistant and asked for my file. I was shocked to see they had a file on me! But he told us every high-ranking employee in the government has such a file. He did not allow me to see the contents, but he made an effort to look through it. With a big smile he told us there was no order for tailing me as there was no reason for it. I did not trust that man's honesty. He was doing his job at a dangerous time with a military government. However, I did notice the tail stopped following me, at least as far as I could tell.

At the time Iraqis were not allowed to take more than eight hundred dinars out of the country. I sent my wife and three-year-old daughter to Germany to stay with her mother and I had sent most of my money with her. A week later I sent a large container that included all our heavy belongings through a well-known transport company, Thomas Cook. In the meantime, a German neighbor in Baghdad, knowing the limits on the amount of money we could take with us, offered to give me a check that his mother had sent from Germany for his children. I was to take it back to Germany and cash it. I felt a one-thousand-dollar German check was not like taking dinars out of the country, and therefore I was not breaking any laws. I paid him for the check a few months later when I was finally working in America.

The night before I was to fly to Tehran to receive my visa from the American Embassy, my family had a few friends stop by to wish me a safe trip. One of our friends, a French businessman, told me he was flying on the same flight with me to Tehran the next day. I thought that was quite a coincidence, and we talked about meeting him there and visiting my cousin who lived in Tehran.

On the day of my flight I arrived at the airport with my brother and his family and was surprised to see seventy to eighty friends, colleagues and extended family waiting to wish me a safe trip. What I also observed was the presence of more than the usual numbers of police and army personnel, including a few captains and majors in full military uniforms with side arms—as though they were expecting a traitor or an attack on the airport.

As I passed a group of them, an officer turned to me and sneered, "Traitor!" Of course, I then realized all those uniforms were there for me. I turned around and whispered to my brother that I was in trouble, and that I needed to get all my documents to the French friend to take to our cousin in Tehran. The documents, apart from my medical reports and x-rays included my correspondence with my new employers in the United States which could have led the government to incriminate me as a doctor abandoning his job.

The passport officer, after looking at my picture, escorted me into a small conference room. My brother had left to talk to the French businessman. In the room there were three army officers waiting. They had my suitcase from the luggage section. They asked me to unlock it which I did. Needless to say, as they foraged through my belongings, I was in a near state of panic.

My friends and family were outside waiting for this situation to be resolved. After the military did not find anything in my bag, they searched my pockets and they found the one-thousand-dollar German check. They wanted to know what that was. I explained the check as described earlier. They sent me to another room while they deliberated. That room was separated from the passenger's room by only a plastic sheet, when I saw the hand of my cousin at the bottom of the sheet, he whispered, "Pass your documents to me." I immediately bent over and slipped him my document folder.

The documents had already been inspected by the low-grade officers who regarded them only as my medical reports. The contents were in English and were too much for them to understand. By the time they released me, my plane had left, and my passport was confiscated. I was told that I could not leave Iraq until a committee in the Central Bank decides that there was no illegal problem. My passport would be kept at the bank until they decided. All the people who came to say good-bye went to my brother's house to celebrate my safety and express sadness about what happened. Too many times they'd seen neighbors, family and friends taken to prison on trumped-up charges.

My brother came to the rescue once more. The following day he went to the bank and vouched for me and assured the bank manager he would come to the hearing in my place. He brought my passport back. I had to wait a couple of days for the next flight to Tehran. My cousin came to the hotel in Tehran and asked me to bring my suitcase. He said, "No cousin of mine will stay in a hotel when I have a house nearby."

The documents were waiting for me there. The kind Frenchman had delivered the envelope as he had promised.

From Tehran I flew to Germany to spend some time with my wife, daughter, and in-laws. We had to go to Munich to get visas for my wife and daughter. From there I flew to New York, with my pregnant wife and young daughter to follow me in one month.

# Chapter Nine

# Life in America

Upon arrival in New York in September 1968, I went to the immigration office. The customs officer asked me if I was carrying any weapons. I told him, "I have a hand gun, and one thousand bullets." He said he had to confiscate both. I presented my booklet from the US Embassy in Tehran and showed him that I had permission to bring my gun. He said he had to call his boss. Both of them stood in amazement that I could actually bring my gun and ammo. The gun was and is still with me. My father gave it to me when I was sixteen.

From New York City, I flew to St. Louis and took a bus to Columbia, Missouri. While waiting for the bus, I bought a cup of coffee at a nearby restaurant, and the waitress brought me what looked like a jar of coffee rather than a cup. I looked at the other tables and everyone had those oversized jar-like cups. It seemed to me that Americans must really like their coffee!

I arrived in Columbia at six p.m. The town was deserted. The shops were closed. There were very few people on the streets. Fortunately, I had a reservation at a hotel and my cab left me there. It was a very strange hotel. Later I learned it was not a highly recommended place, but my bedroom was clean as far as I could tell. I went downstairs to eat but was surprised to know they served no dinners. A hotel staffer told me there was a Dairy Queen restaurant down the street a couple blocks, and that everything else was closed for Labor Day. As I walked to the Dairy Queen, I wondered, what was Labor Day?

Dairy Queen offered only ice cream sandwiches, ice cream cakes, etc. Everything was ice cream. Looking at the dizzying variety, I selected a banana split. I had not seen one before. In Iraq we had our own variety of ice cream, but a banana split was not one of them.

The split came in a large deep plastic plate that boggled my mind. I could not believe one person was expected to eat such a huge amount and didn't believe it possible for me to finish it—even though I had not eaten a thing since breakfast.

While I was struggling with the split, a big, tall American man came over and smiled at me or maybe it was my quickly melting banana split. He must have weighed three hundred pounds, and about six feet four or five. He said, "You're new around here, aren't you?" He offered to shake my hand in that friendly American way. My hand felt lost in that giant hand of his. I'd never seen such a hand in my life. My hand absolutely disappeared from sight in his hand. During our short conversation the giant told me he was a professional football player. To me football was soccer and that man was too big for soccer, so I did not know what he was talking about.

Then I remembered my flight companions flying from New York to St. Louis. A mother and her eleven-year-old son, his excitement about the famous football team in St. Louis had also baffled me.

I began to understand why the coffee is served in jars and the ice cream is served big enough for giants. I concluded Americans are much bigger and taller than Iraqis.

The next day was a workday. All the shops and offices were open, and I had an appointment with Dr. Catanzaro, the CEO of the Mid Missouri Mental Health Center. I took a cab there and his secretary ushered me in. In Iraq a job like that would have a doctor in his fifties as director. The man behind the desk was a tall lean man in his early thirties. He was cheerful but did not seem to take his job seriously. He did not rise to meet me. I was used to the formalities of the Middle East, so, I didn't know if I should sit or stand. He moved his chair back slightly and I thought he was getting up, instead he lifted his legs and put his feet on his desk, as I have since seen men do here. In the old country that position is considered as the ultimate insult that a man can extend to another.

(*While writing this part of my story, I remembered the Iraqi reporter who threw his shoe at President Bush while he was giving a seemingly important speech in Iraq. I don't think the president ever understood what that man was saying to him with his shoe.*)

The CEO then asked me to sit. By then I knew he would not be one of my favorite co-workers. It was even more puzzling when he asked me what my gimmick was. That word was totally new to me and I asked him the meaning of the word. He told me it was colloquial term for "specialty." I told him I had no specialty beside general psychiatry. Then he sent me to his secretary for paperwork.

Despite that initial encounter, I have to say I met a number of colleagues who were very helpful and very friendly. There was a Syrian psychiatrist from Aleppo, the birthplace of my mother. There was another Iraqi who came from Baghdad and there was a Greek doctor who was the head of my unit. There were few American psychiatrists.

One of my unforgettable memories was my third day of work when the Greek doctor asked if I had transportation. I told him I was using the bus. He said, "You have to have a car." I told him that I didn't have the money yet to buy a car. He said, "You don't need money!"

After work he took me to the Chevrolet dealership where a beautiful red Chevrolet Malibu was in the showroom. To make a long story short, I was introduced to the concept of credit. After paying only one hundred dollars down, I left the dealership with a brand-new red Malibu. That was the beginning of my close and long-term relationship with "buying with credit."

After spending two weeks in the hotel, I rented a nice but simple apartment not too far from the hospital. The large crate I had sent from Iraq arrived a week later and the neighbor whom I had befriended helped me move things into the apartment. When my wife and daughter arrived about four weeks later, I had a cozy furnished apartment where we lived for the next year. Our second daughter was born two months after they arrived. The following year we bought a nice home in a residential neighborhood in Columbia. Life was uncomplicated for a while. Our first daughter went to kindergarten and later started school there. The neighborhood was friendly, and my wife found a few friends that she got along with.

Although work was engaging and busy, and I managed to get an extra job on the side to supplement my income, what I made there was not enough to live like we did in Baghdad. I kept my eyes open, looking for a better opportunity.

My work as a psychiatrist was reasonably easy after I learned American ways. Soon I was given a twelve-bed unit to take care of. I started training the residents and the medical students. I began to use electric shock treatment as I had in Baghdad. The only difference was that here I had an anesthetist to put the patient to sleep and give him a muscle relaxant. Both of these procedures were followed in England but not Iraq where we had a shortage of anesthetists and medications. I was given a position at the University of Missouri as an assistant professor because of my training of residents. Two years later I was promoted to professor having submitted to the Department of Psychiatry my research in Iraq and another research paper I published in Missouri.

Sometime at the end of 1972, I received a phone call from Bill Scott, a social worker, who had left Columbia a year before to go to an obscure little town in Pennsylvania. He had worked with me for two years but wanted a new challenge for his career. That call was a life changer for me. Bill invited me to look at a job that entailed establishing psychiatric services in four counties in Northwest Pennsylvania. He said I would be the only psychiatrist there in the beginning and later on I could recruit according to the need.

He told me the only reservation he had was the weather. (At that time, Bradford was known as the Icebox of the nation.) After discussing the offer with my wife, I flew to the area and found the position very enticing even though it was just a small-town set in rural mountains. I went back to Missouri and described what I had seen to my wife. I decided to decline the offer, mainly because of the weather. Bill understood why I was not interested since I lived in Columbia's far more sophisticated environment, and mild winters.

However, he did not give up. He felt I could be the pioneer who could revolutionize everything and create a great legacy when I completed the projects. He then added, "Money was no object." After months of studying the situation and three more trips to Bradford, I reluctantly accepted the position. In September 1973 I moved my family to Bradford; my daughters were five and eight.

All the time I worked taking care of others, I worried about my sister, Nadia. She and her husband had moved to Belgium in 1960 and bought a beautiful apartment in Brussels. While in England I visited her twice, remember. I noticed her lack of emotions, her guardedness and her anxiety. After I came to the US her condition became more serious and I had to go twice to bring her back with me. First to Missouri with my family. She gave me the impression she felt better. Her second visit was to Bradford. Again, she indicated she felt better. However, after these visits, she began writing bizarre letters that were very alarming. She was experiencing delusional and psychotic ideas. She was terrified of imaginary enemies. Her husband took her to a psychiatrist who gave her antipsychotic medications.

However, one day when her husband was at work, she took another overdose. He rushed her to the hospital for treatment. She recovered from that overdose but developed pneumonia. Asked by a nurse if she wanted to live, she said, "Yes." But she died from pneumonia in 1982, she was forty-six years old. Her death was so traumatic for me to accept that to this day her memory haunts me. And I feel the guilt of being a psychiatrist and not being able to save my own sister.

While I worked at the Mid Missouri Mental Health Center, I met a Norwegian psychiatrist named Dr. Terje Fokstuen who was given a fellowship by the Department of Psychiatry. He was assigned to me to supervise. He was there with his wife and three children, who were a little older than our children. The family was gentle and friendly, and we became close friends.

I bring this story up because after finishing his fellowship, the father decided to find employment elsewhere. That was in 1971. In 1983, when I was established in Bradford, I needed to recruit another psychiatrist. Dr. Fokstuen came to mind. I knew he was in Sweden at the time. I called and asked him if he would consider coming to back to the USA. He said yes. He flew over and looked at what we had to offer and accepted the position. For thirty years we worked side by side, and our families have been friends all these years.

My adjustment to my new country was difficult in the beginning. Even though the feelings of inequality and unfairness were not there, instead there was a constant nagging feeling that I should be doing for Iraq what I was doing here. It is not that I was re-inventing the wheel, but I could not ignore the guilt that I felt for having abandoned my country, my family, and my friends. For a long time, I couldn't overcome the constant feeling that I did not belong here. I realized that these feelings were very common to immigrants as they build new lives in foreign lands. It is typically part of the immigration experience.

As the years went by, life continued to be unsatisfactory for my first wife. She was unhappy with me and she was displeased with life in America. After a number of long vacations and one year in Germany she decided to move back to her country. She returned to where she felt more at home. By mutual agreement, we divorced in 1986. Our girls, who were twenty-one and eighteen, stayed with me. They went to college and established successful careers for themselves. Reem lives in Basil, Switzerland. Ban lives in York, Pennsylvania.

In 1988, I was lucky to meet my beautiful wife Cheryl. She worked as a psychiatric nurse at the same unit where I practiced. When I met her father and shook his hand, I couldn't help recalling that first friendly American, the football player who first shook my hand so many years ago—as once again my hand felt lost inside the grip of another American giant. After dating for two years, we were married in July 1990.

Like me she had been married before. Her children Shiela, Sam, and Steve were not too different in age than my children. And so, I became a member of a gracious American family, which at that time included three grandchildren. Cheryl has been a great companion, and partner. She is tireless in taking care of our various needs and interests, as well as her own business. She is an author, in the process of publishing her fourth novel.

Looking back on my life in Iraq, I find that despite many losses along the way, I have been lucky in my journey through the years. The challenges in Iraq were a great preparation for my life in America. It was my destiny to be born where I was and travel far and wide in the world and to finally settle down in a charming small town in the United States of America. It was also my destiny to marry a German lady who left because she was unhappy about her life; and end up married to an American lady who was content with her life. She has filled my life with love, interest and meaning. Having totally lost my family of origin, she brought me into the fold of her strong family of origin.

From Baghdad to Bradford, overall, I have been a lucky man.

# Epilogue

I have reached the end of my story. I hope my readers find it interesting. As I write this last note, I feel very privileged for a man who will be ninety this year. I worked as a psychiatrist at the Guidance Center for forty-five years. The time that is left for me shall be spent in enjoying my family which seems to be constantly expanding. There may be a trip or two still in the cards.

My sister Nadia's death was the saddest and most cruel traumatic experience of my life. Nadia began to complain of loneliness and isolation after moving to Belgium with her husband. She began to have fears of going out; this led to more isolation and paranoia which ended in her final suicide attempt in 1982.

Unfortunately, my very dear friend Dr. Muhammad Ali Khalil, who provided my family with such compassionate care for my mother, passed away in January 2015.

My youngest sister, Ameera, died in 2004, at age sixty-two. She never married; she was a loving and caring woman. She worried about each and every one of us. Ameera had a remarkable memory for names, events, and family history. With her death we lost our connection with the roots of our life. She died of lymphoma which was treated erroneously as sarcoidosis by so-called specialists in England. It was unexpected and tragic.

My brother, Farouq, held many jobs in the government until he decided to form a construction company with
a partner. At one time he was very successful financially
and socially. The change in the political situation in Iraq
and the embargo on the Iraqi people reduced many businesses and lives into a miserable state. He had to sell his
business and leave Iraq for medical care that was no longer
available in the country.

Of course, the war in Iraq destroyed any chance of
recovery for the Iraqi people for decades to come. Farouq
and his loyal wife Hasmeek moved to England to be close
to their daughter. May is married to Majid Al-Warith and
they have three delightful sons: Mazin, Faisal and Saif.
Farouq and Hasmeek's son Laith, married Nisreen. They
have two lovely daughters, Mia and Lara. They live in Abu
Dhabi. Farouq died in 2008, also in England at the age of
seventy-six, of congestive heart failure, which unfortunately had also been misdiagnosed.

Cheryl and I are fortunate to have found each other,
share our lives and to have what we have. She lost her
mother in 2010, at age eighty-four to cancer, despite two
years of chemotherapy. Her father died in 2014, at age
ninety-two of lymphoma, for which he refused to accept any
treatment.

We've been married twenty-nine happy years and
have traveled to more than thirty countries and met many
interesting people from all walks of life. We share five wonderful adult children who by now are all middle-aged. At
this time, we have ten grandchildren, ages fourteen
through thirty-four; and seven great grandchildren, ages

six months through twelve. Experience has taught me, that as a family grows, so do the memories.

Dr. Widad and Cheryl Bazzoui

Ban and Reem with their father, Widad Bazzoui in the USA.

Cheryl and Widad stand beside a replica of the 3000-year-old
Lion of Babylon, a symbol of Babylon's strength. The man
underneath the lion represents the conquered countries.
(The original is in a Middle Eastern museum in London.)

154

Remains of Hathra, about 2000 years old. *Important city in
caravan trade routes to Persia and China.

Widad at remains of Ctesiphon, Al-Madain
(about 2000 years old) near Baghdad.

155

Widad at St Mathew's Monastery, northern Iraq. (Sheikh
Matti) Self-supporting and protected by Saddam Hussein.

Yezzidi cemetery, Ba' Sheeki, northern Iraq, (near Mosul).
Very friendly kind people in that small village.

# Afterword

Forty-nine years ago, I arrived as an immigrant in the United States of America. I have made many attitude adjustments over the years. One of the first was the relationships between the sexes, as well as that between parents and their children. By relationship, I mean all human interactions, restrictions and attitudes that are accepted by society.

My Iraqi heritage went back thousands of years and was deeply influenced by three major religions that have been pervasive in that culture for millenniums. *Culture is a composite of customs, attitudes, and boundaries, in addition to language, art, food and music, etc.* The most conspicuous observation I noted was the openness between the sexes; even more so in the USA than in England. The taboos that regulated interaction between the sexes in the Middle East were nonexistent in my new country. Families arranging marriages was still common in the Middle East, but nearly unheard of in the USA. *Granted I did not choose arranged marriage for myself or my daughters, but it is part of the tapestry of my history.*

Recently when the migrants from the Middle East started flooding Europe, I knew, considering how they were raised—in terms of segregation of the sexes in their culture—it could create problems for European women. They will have difficulty garnering respect from men who are used to women covered up completely and totally out of reach.

The mores and traditions that dictated the acceptable interaction between men and women in the Middle East are the product of thousands of years of social and religious indoctrination. I mentioned earlier in my memoir of the tribal attitude toward women and the need to protect them or recluse them from men, even from their closest male relatives.

Segregation of the sexes was the only way to accomplish protection of women from the roaming eyes and predatory tendencies of men in their tribal tradition. It is still customary in many social systems to see women covered from head to the feet to achieve this end. In the eyes of the Western world it is seen as inhuman and discriminatory. But to those societies it is protective, normative and even religious in meaning. The Western woman has gone over the years from the phase of shrouding attire that we see in historic pictures gradually to the present freedom of attire.

Another adjustment was the relationships of families that I met socially and clinically. In Iraq, the father is supreme and everyone in the family is guided by what he divines. In every society, parents—and in this case fathers—vary in their intelligence, education and personality, but nevertheless, they rule the family. They are respected, looked up to, and sometimes feared. It is commonly said that respect is earned, but back then traditions were endowed.

Looking back at the customs and mores of the old country, religious or tribal, rules were constrictive, unbending and disciplined; assuring security for the tribal leader and even for the tribe or society in general. The rules were meant to provide guidelines and limits where in the old societies there were no enforceable laws. With the advent of the various religions, rules were promulgated for behavior and traditions as ordained by God's doctrines. Within the Western societies, where the disciplines of religious beliefs are gradually dissipating, philosophers and other thinkers are pondering about what can take over this responsibility.

A father is not a buddy but a father, that phenomenon initially impressed me as cute but unusual. For many years I wondered how this diverted relationship would affect the family and overall society. Law and order, the instruments of governments, are reluctantly and often unsuccessfully replacing the old rules. Since there is no way law and order can reach the inner transactions of family life, it appears to be far less effective in delineating the boundaries of social interaction.

One can easily see that humanity left with or without nebulous guidance will extend its freedoms ad infinitum. So, over the years, as I became accustomed to my new world, I have worried that the borders drawn here to guide and control human nature are becoming less adequate to do the job.

It is not yet fair to say that we are living in a society where anything goes or is permissible, but we are heading there. It appears to me that the seers of this world are going to have to sit in pow-wows as humans did hundreds of years ago to find a new system to regulate relationships on our Earth. Religion is slowly on the way out, the tribal system is no longer tenable, law and order are inadequate, men and women are gradually becoming equal, and governments have too much to attend to, to bother. So, what are we going to do?

Another adjustment I found myself facing is the pace of humans in the United States. The Middle East is a very warm climate. Life goes at a much slower pace. Running is on the whole, not a healthy pursuit. In Iraq people take a siesta from about two p.m. until four p.m. in the summer and sometimes all year round. They are not in a hurry because one gets easily exhausted in the heat. The pressure of this fast pace is different. Not only that, but there is always tomorrow. There is less pressure and more introspection or pondering. Of course, I had to learn all the rules and ways of America to feel that I am an American. I have had to train myself to work after lunch. After fifty-one years without a siesta, I still miss it.

I finally retired on December 31, 2018, and I have happily returned to my afternoon siestas.

# Acknowledgments

This memoir is a work of love; all my stories are true according to my memories. I thank all members of my nuclear birth family for the memories... since I am the last one standing; none of them can tell me I got something wrong. I miss them every day and only wish they were still here to correct my stories and add their own.

Thank you to my early readers, who proofed and made constructive comments: Cheryl, Maureen Johnson, Ingrid Fokstuen, Susan Anderson, Edie Hanes, Lee Beckes, and Dr. Dick Dryden. And to my extraordinary editor, Cynthia Moyer. You're all my writing community and you helped make my memoir become a better book. I appreciate all your efforts, suggestions, and encouragement.

I thank my wife, Cheryl, for her diligence in seeing that I complete my story. Whenever I'd share one of my old tales, she'd say, "Write that down, that's not in your memoir and it should be!" That is how my memories slowly grew into a book. I thank her for her patience and assistance with the manuscript. Without her, I don't believe my memoir would have reached completion.

And I humbly thank the readers who took time to read about a time that is forever gone in a faraway land that was *my first home.*

Widad E. Bazzoui, M.D.

Dr. Widad E. Bazzoui

Made in the USA
Middletown, DE
19 July 2019